EX LIBRIS

The choreography of the kitchen—I peel, you scrape, wine spills, bag splits, beans simmer, sink slurps, petals fall, flour drifts, crust splits, aromas spread, lights flicker, chocolate melts, glass shatters, sauce thickens, finger bleeds, cheese ripens, crumbs fall, sweat drips, spoon bangs, meat glistens, oil spatters, wine breathes, garlic smashes, lettuces float, silver shines, apron snags, you sneeze, I sing oh, my love, my darling, and dough rises in soft moons the size of my cupped hand as planet earth tilts us toward dinner.

—FROM *Every Day in Tuscany*

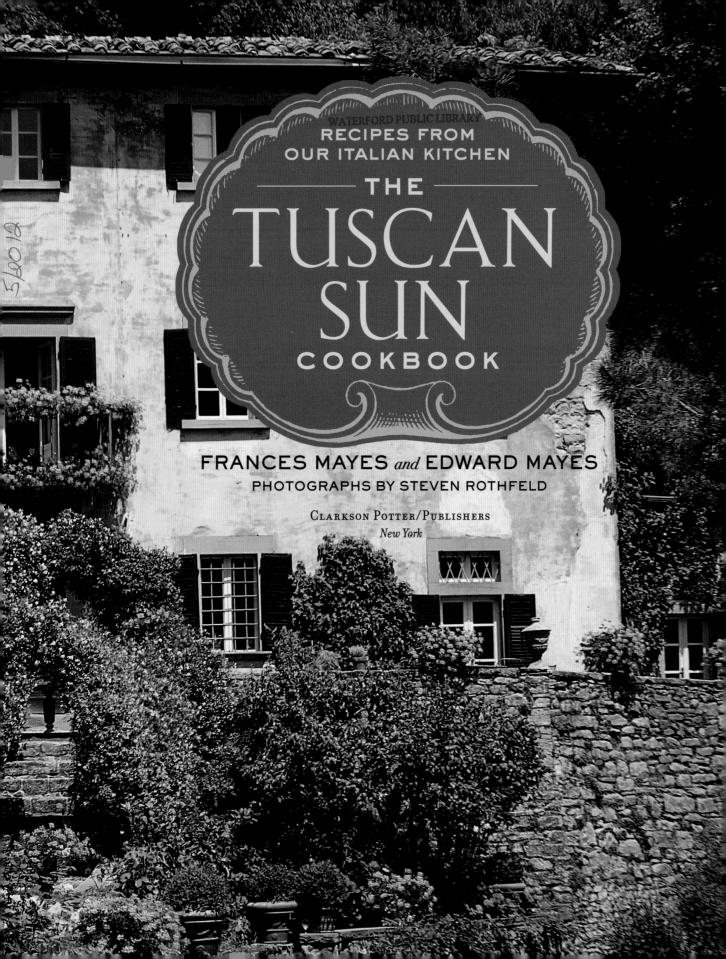

RECIPES FROM
OUR ITALIAN KITCHEN

THE

TUSCAN
SUN

COOKBOOK

FRANCES MAYES and **EDWARD MAYES**

PHOTOGRAPHS BY STEVEN ROTHFELD

Clarkson Potter/Publishers
New York

DEDICATION

This book is one long toast, *cin-cin*, to near and dear Tuscan friends, who have shared their creative improvisations on passed-down, hallowed recipes. Early in our time here, we met Giuseppina De Palme, called Giusi. A natural cook, she is a mother of two who lives far in the country in a *casa colonica* with her husband and his parents. Her family feasts initiated us into the eight-hour meals so common in the Tuscan countryside. She now owns her own idyllic *agriturismo*, but she continues to invite us to lavish feasts. Her generosity and her passion for cooking inspire every meal we prepare. Later, we met Gilda Di Vizio, Giusi's sister-in-law. She is equally inventive and accomplishes more in a morning than I can in a day. She brings us armfuls of sunflowers, meat from her livestock, jars of fig jam, and baskets of zucchini flowers because she knows we *americani* adore them

fried. Gilda's life force, raucous sense of humor, and earthmother knowledge of the land all brighten the skies over Cortona.

As we got to know our neighbors and their friends, we felt the inexpressible joy of being included on a regular basis in the rounds of celebration that define the days of the local people. Our friends are cooks, engineers, winemakers, plumbers, gym teachers, woodcutters, doctors, *fashionistas*, electricians, police chiefs, writers, and the local aristocracy. As foreigners, we are freed from the bounds of profession and class. We eat everywhere—in the contessa's frescoed villa and the sheepherder's stone cottage.

During our years here, we have accumulated notebooks of recipes from our friends and from *trattorie* and restaurants where we eat regularly. Placido

Cardinali and Fiorella Badini, our neighbors, are the truest gourmands I have met. I would like to have a head count of the number of people they entertain every year. When Ed is in Italy

without me, Fiorella walks over and says, "I hope you're not thinking of eating dinner alone. That's not good for you." He finds himself over at La Casita every night, with Plari, as her husband is called, grilling sausages, or a pigeon he's raised behind the

house, and Fiorella making the tagliatelle.

The stylish and fun Baracchi family, Riccardo and his wife, Silvia Regi, with their son Benedetto, own the sybaritic country inn and restaurant Il Falconiere. The hospitality of the family reveals the depth of their natural joy in living. What feasts they produce! I was flattered when Silvia named her school "Cooking Under the Tuscan Sun." Silvia is a cutting-edge chef with intact, deep country roots. Whatever I think I know how to do, Silvia can knock it up a notch. Their inn is a second home for us. Riccardo makes highly prized wines and a Champagne-method

sparkling wine that inspires Ed to write sonnets.

Our connections to the place multiplied a few years ago when we restored a twelfth-century stone house, Fonte delle Foglie (Font of Leaves) on Monte Sant'Egidio. There we have an ever-expanding vegetable garden and orchard. We gather chestnuts from the forest, fight the invasive wild boar constantly, and love the owl calls at night. The lights of Cortona in the distance seem far away from our mountain perch.

During the long restoration, we built a bread oven and grill near the kitchen. Our neighbors, Domenica Italiani and her exuberant son, Ivan, taught us the mysteries of our brick-domed oven and how to turn out 30 to 40—once we even made 65—pizzas for hungry guests. Domenica has

an outdoor kitchen at her house, where she constantly bottles tomatoes, puts up wild cherries, and makes vats of quince and fig jams. Ivan, a trained chef, makes scrumptious desserts and sometimes drops off a blackberry crostata at Fonte. Do they taste better because they've baked in a wood-fired oven? I like to stop by their house because there's always something to taste on their red wood-fired stove and Domenica is likely to be rolling out the pasta for lunch. The tiny grandmother Annette goes out to gather eggs. Ivan rushes in from his job and dives right in. The noise level rises, the scents of baking rabbit, sizzling pancetta, and lemon tart crowd the kitchen. The Italiani in the kitchen—all's well in the world.

Cin-cin, my friends, and *mille grazie.*

CONTENTS

LA CUCINA *9*

KEYS TO THE PANTRY *17*

ANTIPASTI *35*

PRIMI *63*

SECONDI *111*

CONTORNI *151*

DOLCI *177*

APERITIVI E DIGESTIVI *213*

ACKNOWLEDGMENTS *219*

INDEX *220*

LA CUCINA

If you came to visit me in Tuscany, we would cook the food described in this book. *The Tuscan Sun Cookbook* collects our favorite recipes from hundreds of dinners here at our home Bramasole, from the tables of our generous friends, and from chefs whose kitchens are as familiar to us as our own. Along with the food, Tuscans add to the table the spirit of friendship and their legendary sense of exuberance. We have feasted for over two decades in this profoundly hospitable country.

Etruscan tombs from 800 B.C. show men and women reclining around the banquet table. Their archaic faces reflect the joys of dining that are cherished in Italy—and have been forever. No matter what the circumstances, life is meant to be enjoyed, and what better place than around a laden table surrounded by friends and family?

Tuscan food tastes like itself. Ingredients are left to shine, not combined with a list as long as your arm or tortured into odd combinations. So, if on your visit, I hand you an apron, your work will be easy. We'll start

with *primo* ingredients, a little flurry of activity, perhaps a glass of Vino Nobile di Montepulciano, and soon we'll be carrying platters out the door. We'll have as much fun setting the table as we have in the kitchen. Four double doors along the front of the house open to the outside—so handy for serving at a long table under the stars (or for cooling a scorched pan on the stone wall). Italian Philosophy 101: *la casa aperta,* the open house. Inside / outside living seems natural.

In cool weather, we'll light many candles and dine at the oval table in the dining room, where so many years ago we discovered a fresco under the whitewash.

What Shall We Cook?
We'll *assemble* most of the antipasti—the pecorino, various slices of salami, prosciutto and melon, some vegetables *sott'olio* (under olive oil), breadsticks or wedges of focaccia—these we've simply gathered. But we'll quickly fry some delectable zucchini flowers lightly stuffed with a spoon of whipped potato and some basil. We've added a mound of chickpeas with curls of lemon zest, and perhaps a chopped radicchio salad

with pecorino. The platters are gorgeous and travel quickly around the table. Next, for our *primo*, we'll throw together spaghetti *all'arrabbiata*—Angry Pasta—which Tuscans love for its hit of vibrant hot pepper. This simple pasta will rev up our taste buds.

Two courses so far and an hour has passed. We pause a little before the *secondo* because there's no rush and the moon is just now wobbling up over the distant hills. *Scottaditi* are forthcoming—finger-burners, they're named, because the little lamb chops are quickly seared on the grill and the bone is hot. Two small chops, some bitter greens, and *basta*, that's it for the *secondo*. Bread of course, but nothing more. Meat is important to the Tuscan meal but it is not the main course. There is no main course—all are equal. You have, in this lovely sequence, a chance to savor each. Out comes a bowl of fruit and then another bowl of water to wash it in. A wedge of cheese. We pause for a while, sipping the wine and changing chairs so everyone can visit everyone else.

We could stop there, and Tuscans do, but tonight you will be pleased to carry aloft from the kitchen a huge rustic tart of peaches. I'll pass around some sweetened mascarpone to spoon on top. We're into our

third hour and in another, guests will begin to go home because it is, after all, a Wednesday night. Some linger longer because Ed brings out a tray of *digestivi*. I'm partial to the golden Strega from Benevento, in the south. Ed is convincing everyone to try the *amaro* (bitter) made from olives that we brought home from the Marche. Fulvio prefers the Cocchi Barolo Chinato, a spicy quinine concoction with a base of Barolo. Over the wall go the orange peels and grape seeds. Finally, the rounds of two-cheek kissing and the calls of *buonanotte* begin as everyone starts toward home.

When We Came Here

What a thrill it was to find, finally, genuine Italian food. Right away, when the first primitive kitchen at Bramasole consisted only of a door on sawhorses, a stove, and hot water hauled from the bathroom, I found that by reproducing the pastas and salads we were tasting at *trattorie* in town, I was able to prepare a fine dinner in under an hour. *La cucina povera*, the poor kitchen, became a source of study. What the old signoras who previously owned Bramasole did in the lean times was a wonder to me. The cuisine of necessity—how inventive they were with

their tomato and bread soups, their *tortellini in brodo*, their *panzanella* (bread salad), and their bean dishes. I was fascinated by their habit of cooking beans in a bottle in the hot ashes of the fireplace. The chestnut cake of the region, *castagnaccio*, a strange, flat concoction of chestnut flour, olive oil, and rosemary—surely an acquired taste—charmed me with its honesty.

At Bramasole

Ed lavishes care on our original 160 olive trees, and has acquired another grove just below us, adding another 250 trees—another 250 bottles. Yes, a bottle a tree! Although the yield varies each year, our average is a liter a tree. The trees must be pruned, the land plowed, the olives picked, taken to the mill, pressed, and bottled. The harvest is a labor of true love.

Naturally, Tuscan food almost always involves a drizzle or a blast of this tender elixir. Alessio Burroni at our local *gelateria* even made gelato from our olive oil and we served it at the annual Tuscan Sun Festival. Extra-virgin olive oil is the key to the taste of Italian food. My first recommendation is to find an excellent one and use it liberally. Here's the great secret: the food will be so tasty, so satisfying, that you will not require huge portions of it. Ed works with six men—three in their eighties—to harvest and prune. They taught him to cut so that the *upupa*, hoopoe, can fly through without brushing their wings against the limbs. As in the kitchen, we have had the grand luck to have such friends, whose love of the natural world connects them solidly to it. This tribe of friends shows us, by example, the happiness of every day in this *bellissima* landscape.

Ed fell hard for cooking here. He'd always had his specialties—soufflés and soups and swordfish with mango salsa—but he was the sous chef, who chopped the onions and asked me for directions. Now he's the one who makes the pasta, gnocchi, and long-simmered *ragù*. Together, we took naturally to the Italian sense of hospitality. While in Italy, we have eight or ten friends over at least twice a week. For our Twenty Years at Bramasole party we threw a grand dinner for forty-five and Silvia orchestrated the feast. We have so many houseguests that we could open our own inn. It's fun until they leave and we face a mountain of laundry. On weekends in the mountains, guests swim, hike, and play bocce. Then eat! Our bread oven turns out the pizzas, then the *pasta al forno* and roasted chickens. The wine flows and the music wraps around us. A chill falls at night. We build a fire in the outdoor grill. I run into the house and bring out shawls and sweaters and we draw near the warmth because it's a summer night and Antonio has brought his guitar. Ed and Alberto break out the bitters, especially Averna, a dark and syrupy liquid made from thirty-two herbs. I like the clear purity of grappa but cannot take more than a sip because it seems like a glass of it would tip over my chair.

Food! The obsession of every Tuscan. Since others also entertain frequently, we fall into constant musical chairs at each other's houses, but despite the camaraderie at table, we enjoy our private dinners at home the most—grilling veal chops in the fireplace, gathering vegetables from the garden, and improvising a frittata, or discovering a new sauce for pasta.

Many Friends Inspire Us

With many friends, we run around in the countryside visiting vineyards, butchers, cheese makers, and old people who like to sit by the fire, sip vin santo, and talk about Tuscany as it was. Everyone has a story—and most of the stories involve food.

We hope that our kitchen's bounty, too, will inspire you to say, "That looks good."

Most recipes are simple and the few that are not are fun. This is real Tuscan food from a small hill town we have grown to love as home. Because of our many years here, we've had the great luck to learn about Tuscan food from the inside, not as visitors. Although we enjoy the new ideas and trends now cropping up in Italy, this book focuses on traditional fare and on the spontaneity of cooks working within their legacy. Sometimes we add a few twists of our own. What I hope becomes real for you is the astonishing range of Tuscan food, and the sense of joy that permeates the Tuscan kitchen. No one I know considers weeknight dinner after work a pain. Cooking is a natural act, like taking a shower.

If you are visiting me, we will go to the enormous weekly market in the morning. I have my favorite stands for the little violet artichokes, a *porchetta* sandwich to eat while shopping, fish from the Adriatic, and Casa Blanca lilies for your room. We'll pause for an espresso. The car will fill with the scent of cantaloupe and fennel and grapes. Then we'll come home, laden with bottles and bags, and after lunch, we'll start all over again.

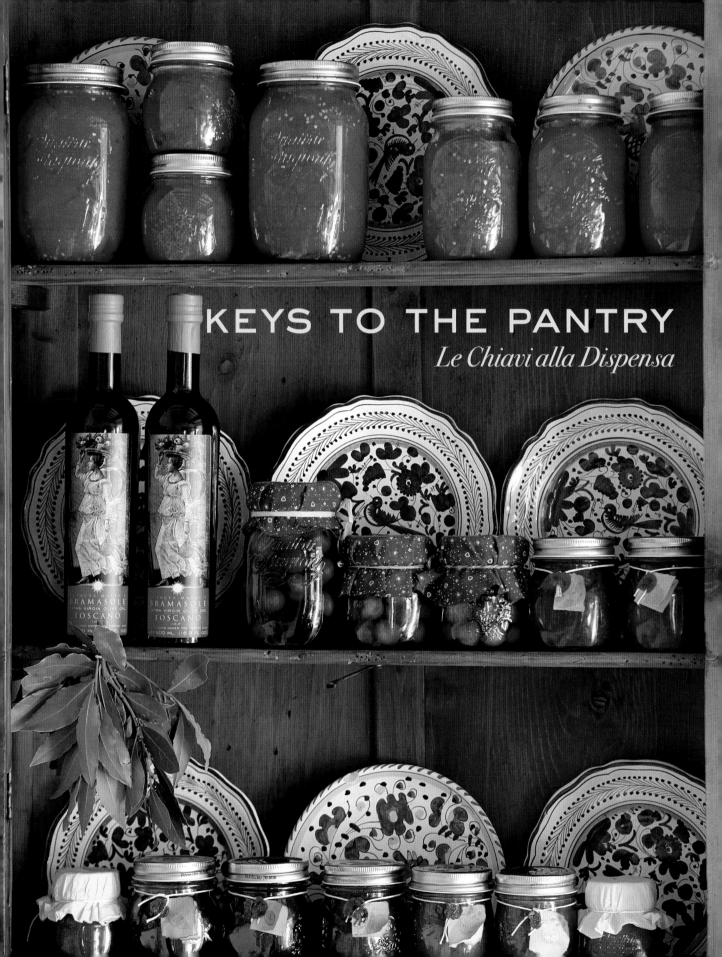

KEYS TO THE PANTRY
Le Chiavi alla Dispensa

Tuscan recipes usually call for few ingredients—that's why you don't spend the day in the kitchen when you're having a few people over. But there's another secret to the ease of Tuscan food: *la dispensa*, the pantry. Does the word call up images of a medical supply room in the tropics? Despite the clinical sound, a stocked *dispensa* is the glory of the Tuscan kitchen. Seeing our pantry shelves lined with jars of cherries and peaches gives me ideas when contemplating winter desserts. Fiorella puts up eggplant and Placido dries mushrooms in the autumn sun. Ed packs fresh anchovies in salt, and lets them rest for three months in a covered bowl. Ivan is king of our blackberry-invaded mountainside. He bestows on us jars of fig, quince, apple, and plum preserves. Roll out a piecrust, spread the jam, and there's a *crostata*, Tuscany's favorite tart. These enterprises make all the difference—and sharing with friends is part of the pleasure. Every time I open a jar of Gilda's boar sausage, I think of her. Ivan's quince jam reminds me of his big smile.

This is the late August ritual: With help from Gilda and Domenica, we put up two hundred jars of fresh tomatoes and at least thirty of *pomarola*, simmered tomato sauce. Although I keep fresh herbs growing all year, I still dry rosemary, marjoram, fennel flowers, thyme, sage, and oregano when they flourish. That's an easy task. Pick a basketful of herbs, stem and all, and spread them on a rack. Just let them rest in a warm, dry place for four days, then strip the leaves and store them in small jars. They will be on hand for seasoning until next summer, when I hope to do the same thing again.

Tuscans are foragers. In every season, people are in the fields looking for whatever is springing up—porcini, wild cherries, chestnuts, field greens, fennel flowers, wild asparagus, green almonds, and berries, especially the ruby-drop wild strawberries. Preserving, I think, comes from the same hunter-gatherer instinct that sends my neighbors out at midnight to look for snails on the walls of a brooding castle. The finding and the keeping—both impulses reveal the deep Tuscan connection to the land.

With a well-stocked *dispensa*, your planning, shopping, and cooking times are shortened. Here are some ingredients to have on hand in your kitchen:

ALMONDS, SLICED AND WHOLE

BAY LEAVES

BALSAMIC VINEGAR

CAPERS

CARNAROLI, VIALONE NANO, OR
ARBORIO RICE

CHEESES: PARMIGIANO-REGGIANO,
FONTINA, TALEGGIO, PECORINO
(FRESH, SLIGHTLY AGED, AND
AGED), GORGONZOLA, ROBIOLA,
ASIAGO, GRANA PADANO

DRIED CHICKPEAS, CANNELLINI
BEANS, ZOLFINO BEANS, FARRO

DRIED PORCINI

FENNEL SEEDS AND FENNEL
FLOWERS

HONEY, FROM LAVENDER, ACACIA,
OR TIGLI (LINDEN)

HAZELNUTS

OLIVES, GREEN AND BLACK

EXTRA-VIRGIN OLIVE OIL, THE
FRESHEST YOU CAN FIND

PEPERONCINI (RED PEPPER
FLAKES)

PINOLI (PINE NUTS)

PISTACHIOS

ANCHOVIES, SALT-PACKED OR OIL-
PACKED

SAFFRON

SEA SALT, COARSE

SEMOLINA

POLENTA

WALNUTS

FRA ANGELICO

LIMONCELLO

VIN SANTO

DRY CINZANO

Most Tuscan kitchens do not have the battery of "toys" that we take for granted in the United States. Their cooking equipment is light and flimsy by our standards. My friends look askance at our big food processor and say, "It's usually faster in the long run to use your own two hands." Privately, I often use that scorned food processor to make a quick pasta. Also, the pasta attachment for a mixer is handy when you want to make fusilli, macaroni, rigatoni, or bucatini. You can't make those shapes with a traditional pasta machine or by hand.

Our early months here revolutionized my thinking. From that kitchen with a door on two sawhorses, a stove, tiny fridge, and one wooden spoon, we were feasting like kings. I had to learn that I really didn't need fourteen knives and cupboards filled with pans. It was also during that primitive-kitchen era that I learned the most valuable lesson ever: double the recipe. I still double. Or triple, especially with ragù. It just makes sense for busy people.

Most of our recipes take the hands-on approach, but of course, we use mixers, food processor, hand blender, meat thermometers, microwave, and mandoline when we want. We also recommend:

HAND-CRANKED PASTA MACHINE

MEZZALUNA AND WOODEN BOWL FOR CHOPPING

MORTAR AND PESTLE

LEMON ZESTER AND PEELER

ROTARY PIZZA CUTTER

SPRINGFORM PANS

POULTRY SHEARS

STRAIGHT ROLLING PIN (NOT TAPERED)

FOOD MILL

NUTMEG GRATER

Wine Suggestions

For many recipes, we suggest excellent wines that we regularly serve and enjoy. We've chosen only ones with wide distribution. If you can't find the suggested one, thousands of others are available. Many good choices on your wine seller's shelves will be stellar matches for your goose or baked pasta. Just after the right butcher, a good wine merchant should be your second-best friend. If she is knowledgeable, she always can find some similar bottles—or maybe something better!

ESSENTIALS OF THE TUSCAN KITCHEN

A few elemental recipes are used over and over in the Tuscan kitchen. Because they occur often, we're including them at the outset. You might want to tag these pages so when you come to a cross-reference, you can turn right to them.

THE BASICS

SOFFRITTO *20*

TOMATO SAUCE *21*

FOCACCIA *23*

DRIED CANNELLINI BEANS AND CHICKPEAS *24*

BESCIAMELLA *24*

GILDA'S SALT *24*

BRINE *25*

PESTO *26*

SOFFRITTO

A quick sauté of carrot, onion, celery, and flat-leaf parsley starts off many sauces and meats. The greengrocer usually will ask as you finish your shopping, "Do you need *odori*?" And he will hand you a bunch of these "smells" to make *soffritto*. The word is from *soffriggere*, to cook at a below-frying temperature. *Soffritto*, similar to *mirepoix* in France, is lightly fried *odori*. Depending on the recipe, you can add a variety of other ingredients to the *soffritto*: 2 minced cloves of garlic, ¼ pound of minced pancetta, 4 or 5 torn basil leaves, or other aromatic herbs. Use this in *ragù* or soup and as a seasoning for zucchini, peas, or other vegetables. Mix some with breadcrumbs and stuff tomatoes with it. When I add a cup of chopped, oven-roasted tomatoes to a *soffritto*, I can serve forth a perfect *sugo* for Sunday night spaghetti.

We frequently prepare a big batch, let it cool, and freeze ½ cup portions in small plastic bags. They're then ready when I'm on a mission for a fast dinner. MAKES 1 CUP

- ¼ CUP EXTRA-VIRGIN OLIVE OIL
- 1 YELLOW ONION, MINCED
- 1 CARROT, MINCED
- 1 CELERY STALK, MINCED
- 1 HANDFUL OF FLAT-LEAF PARSLEY, MINCED
- ½ TEASPOON SALT
- ¼ TEASPOON PEPPER

Sauté the ingredients in a small saucepan over medium-low heat until they begin to color and turn tender, 5 to 7 minutes.

TOMATO SAUCE

Pomarola—classic and omnipresent. For true fast food: ¼ cup of *pomarola* per person, stirred into pasta, a wave over the plate with Parmigiano, a few torn basil leaves, and here it is!—*eccolo*! This is the food for which homesick Italian travelers yearn. Some even travel with *pelati*, cans of Italian tomatoes, so they can whip up a meal redolent of home. You can add garlic, thyme, oregano, or pepper flakes if you like, but this recipe is for plain and authentic *pomarola*. Use fresh, boxed, or canned tomatoes (juice included), peeled or not, as you prefer. Canned and boxed tomatoes generally are peeled. I usually don't peel fresh tomatoes. For sauces, the San Marzano variety is the Italian choice. The sauce will keep in the fridge for about a week. MAKES 3 CUPS

- ¼ CUP EXTRA-VIRGIN OLIVE OIL
- 1 YELLOW ONION, MINCED
- 8 TOMATOES OR 1 28-OUNCE CAN WHOLE TOMATOES, COARSELY CHOPPED
- 8 TO 10 BASIL LEAVES, TORN
- ½ TEASPOON SALT
- ⅓ TEASPOON PEPPER

In a medium saucepan, heat the olive oil over medium heat and add the onion. Sauté for about 5 minutes, until golden and soft. Add the tomatoes, basil, salt, and pepper. Bring the sauce to a boil, then immediately lower the heat to a brisk simmer and cook, uncovered, stirring occasionally, for 10 minutes, or until glossy and thickened.

FOCACCIA

What better place to focus on some focaccia than the *focolare*, hearth or fireplace, which could very well be the root word of this bread's name. Focaccia is simple, requires few ingredients, and everybody likes it.

During the grape harvest, the breakfast or *merenda*, snack, of choice is focaccia baked with small, sugared grapes on top. In winter, I cannot resist focaccia baked with caramelized onions. Of course, focaccia makes the best *panini*.

To grill or not? Usually in Tuscany a *panino* is not grilled and there are no condiments. The olive oil in the focaccia suffices. I love grilled *panini*, too, especially in winter.

SERVES 8

- 2 PACKAGES ACTIVE DRY YEAST
- 2 CUPS WARM WATER (110° TO 115°F)
- 5 TO 5½ CUPS ALL-PURPOSE FLOUR, SIFTED, PLUS ADDITIONAL FOR THE WORK SURFACE
- 2 TABLESPOONS EXTRA-VIRGIN OLIVE OIL
- 1½ TEASPOONS COARSE SEA SALT
- 2 TABLESPOONS MINCED FRESH ROSEMARY OR 1 TABLESPOON DRIED

Combine the yeast and water in a large bowl. After 10 minutes, gradually add 5 cups of flour and, with a fork, mix well. On a generously floured surface, knead the dough for 10 to 15 minutes, adding the other ½ cup flour as needed, until the dough is uniformly elastic. Swab a large bowl with a tablespoon of the olive oil, add the dough, and turn to coat all sides with the oil. Cover the bowl with a dishtowel and put it in a warm place for 1 hour.

Punch down the dough—it should have almost doubled—then, with your fingers, spread it to fit a parchment-lined 13 x 18-inch sheet pan. Cover again with the dishtowel and let it rise in a warm place for 45 minutes.

Preheat the oven to 400°F.

With your fingertips, dimple the dough all over. Dribble the remaining 1 tablespoon of olive oil over the top and sprinkle with the salt and rosemary.

Bake for 20 minutes. Cool slightly before slicing.

FAVORITE PANINI

Roasted vegetables and grana padano

———

Grilled eggplant, mozzarella, and tomato

———

Finocchiona *salami and fontina*

———

Anchovy and butter

———

Taleggio and tomato

———

Grilled chicken and sage

———

Arugula, prosciutto, and Gorgonzola

———

Mortadella and provolone

DRIED CANNELLINI BEANS AND CHICKPEAS

How to cook them? This is the easiest way: Soak them at least 5 hours, and bring them to a boil in abundant water. Add a carrot, a celery stalk, and a halved onion, if you like. Lower the heat, partially cover, and simmer until done—and you just keep testing for that. The cooking time might be as short as 45 minutes, if the beans or chickpeas are young. Test frequently; when done, they should be firm but giving. Discard the vegetables. Add seasonings to taste.

There are other options with no soaking at all—boil the beans or chickpeas for 2 minutes and then turn off the heat and let them sit for an hour before cooking. Or, just cook them. You may have to check on them for longer than you want but eventually they will be done.

BESCIAMELLA

Besciamella, béchamel sauce, is a basic white sauce for vegetables and baked pastas. You can add ½ cup of cheese, depending on the recipe. The cheese could be Parmigiano-Reggiano for a vegetable sauce or the filling in cannelloni, or Gorgonzola for a savory pasta sauce with walnuts and garlic. MAKES 1 CUP

- 2 TABLESPOONS UNSALTED BUTTER
- 2 TABLESPOONS ALL-PURPOSE FLOUR
- 1 CUP WHOLE MILK
  A FEW GRATINGS OF NUTMEG
- ½ TEASPOON SALT

Over medium-low heat, melt the butter in a 1½-quart saucepan and add the flour. Cook, stirring for 2 minutes, until it forms a paste and is ever-so-slightly browned. Remove from the heat and whisk in the milk all at once. Return to medium-low heat and cook, stirring until thickened, about 5 minutes. Add the nutmeg and salt. If you're using cheese, stir it in at the end, and let the sauce heat on low until the cheese has melted and absorbed.

GILDA'S SALT

Gilda keeps a jar of her seasoned salt by the stove. If she's roasting meat, she rubs it all over with her salt and leaves it in the fridge overnight, kind of a dry brining system. I've used other salts, but hers is different—the fresh garlic and lemon give a punch of flavor. We give jars of this as small gifts.
MAKES ABOUT 4 CUPS

- 1½ CUPS FRESH ROSEMARY
- 1½ CUPS FRESH SAGE LEAVES
- 1 CUP GARLIC CLOVES
- ½ LEMON, SEEDED, CUT INTO 4 PIECES
- 1 SMALL BAY LEAF
- 3 TABLESPOONS PEPPER
- 2½ CUPS FINE SEA SALT

Put the rosemary, sage, garlic, lemon, bay leaf, and pepper in a food processor, and pulse until minced and blended. Add the salt and pulse a few more times until everything is well mixed. Store in jars.

BRINE

Brining makes meats more succulent and flavorful and it's a simple process—water, salt, and sugar. In Tuscany, brining is not done usually, except with game meat, but I frequently brine pork roast, whole chickens, and turkey. The following recipe is for pork. For a chicken, halve the amounts and brine for 2 hours in the fridge. Meat that's brined too long changes texture. For a turkey, double or triple the amounts, depending on the size of the bird, and brine overnight.

- 1 GALLON HOT WATER
- ½ CUP SALT
- ½ CUP SUGAR

Fill a large bowl or roasting pan with the water. Pour in the salt and sugar and stir to dissolve. When the water cools, add the pork loin, cover, and refrigerate for at least 6 hours. Wash the pork under cold running water, dry it with paper towels, and proceed.

BALSAMIC VINEGAR

Aceto Balsamico Tradizionale di Modena (or Reggio Emilia) has spent at least 12 years aging in wood. Some rare vinegars have aged for 150 years. If you see *"extra-vecchio"* on the bottle, the vinegar is a minimum of 25 years old. These are marvelous flavor enhancers to use sparingly. When I come home from Italy, I tuck a beautiful little bottle in my luggage. Expect to pay dearly for these *primo* balsamics.

For daily use, *condimento balsamico* is what sits next to the other vinegars in my kitchen. This can be sold before 12 years in the casks and may be from outside the recognized and protected region. Let taste guide you; some are excellent.

The third category, Aceto Balsamico di Modena, varies in quality. The advice on olive oil goes for balsamic vinegar, too—buyer beware. This grade of balsamic vinegar will be a combination of reduced grape juice, vinegar, and sometimes caramel. I'd avoid one with caramel added to it.

The longer *aceto balsamico* has aged, the more concentrated—and expensive—it is. I keep a 6-year one for cooking purposes and a fine older one for a salad and fruit condiment. With the best, try a couple of drops on a veal chop, duck breast, vanilla ice cream, rasp-berries, pears, pineapple, or strawberries.

PESTO

So easy a small child can make it, pesto is a very good friend, not only for pasta but also for *crostini*, baked chicken, shrimp, pizza, or a sandwich condiment. If you raise basil, keep pinching off the white flowers. (They make a fragrant garnish.) Harvest your crop at its peak and make batches of pesto to freeze in small jars after topping them with olive oil. You can keep it in the freezer for 6 months.

Pesto comes together instantly in a food processor, but it's such a pleasure to make it with a mortar and pestle. Mine was originally used to grind salt and I rescued it from a friend who flicked cigarette ashes into it.

MAKES 1¾ CUPS

1	LARGE BUNCH BASIL (ABOUT 5 CUPS), CURLY GENOVESE IF AVAILABLE, WASHED AND DESTEMMED
4	GARLIC CLOVES
½	TEASPOON SALT
½	TEASPOON PEPPER
¼	CUP PINE NUTS
¾	CUP EXTRA-VIRGIN OLIVE OIL
½	CUP (2 OUNCES) GRATED PARMIGIANO-REGGIANO

With a rotating motion, crush the basil leaves, garlic, salt, and pepper against the sides of the mortar. Add the pine nuts and continue to smear against the side. Slowly incorporate the olive oil. When a thick, dark green sauce has formed, stir in the Parmigiano.

Or, toss everything but the olive oil and Parmigiano into the food processor, whir until blended, then slowly incorporate the olive oil and pulse in the cheese. Use the pesto immediately or scrape it into a bowl, spread a layer of olive oil on top, cover, and refrigerate for up to 4 days.

Dried Porcini

Barely cover the dried mushrooms with tepid water, white wine, or *vin santo*. Let them steep until pliable, about 30 minutes. Filter the liquid through cheesecloth or a fine sieve. The liquid probably will be used in the recipe. If not, add it to a soup or a *ragù*. Squeeze out the liquid from the mushrooms and chop or leave them in large pieces.

Saffron

To make the most of saffron's color and flavor, soak the threads in a tablespoonful of tepid water for 1 hour, and then add both the threads and the water to what you're cooking.

Mozzarella

Whether the water buffaloes arrived in Italy courtesy of the Arabs, Goths, or Normans remains unknown. What *is* known is that for centuries, Italians have adored the fresh, soft *mozzarella di bufala* made from rich buffalo milk. The moist and most delicate cheese is sliced for salads or, in *bocconcini*, tiny balls, on antipasto plates. Fresh artisan mozzarella, whether made from buffalo or cow milk, is terrific to top a savory tart, as a snack on *bruschetta*, snipped into pasta sauces, or slipped inside something fried, such as Sicilian *arancini* and Roman *supplì*, both crunchy fried rice balls.

For pizza topping and many vegetable dishes, low-moisture mozzarella, sold in 8-ounce "bricks," is generally preferred.

Anchovies

Fresh anchovies, *alici*, marinated in lemon juice and vinegar, are readily available in Tuscany, and frequently are featured as part of an antipasto platter. Anchovies are as omnipresent as garlic and olive oil. They provide in their invisibility (since they disappear shortly after hitting hot oil in a pan) a taste that stimulates the flavors of so many other ingredients. Since fresh anchovies are quite difficult to find in the United States, our recipes call for preserved anchovies, *acciughe*. Use either salt-packed and bone-in, or oil-packed fillets.

Citrus Zest

Make sure your lemons and oranges are organic if you are planning on cooking with the peel.

Garnishes

Part of the play of cooking is setting the table with candles and flowers and place cards. Garnishing the dishes may be gilding the lily, but it's fun. Besides the usual sliced lemons or oranges, these are other favorites: pomegranate seeds, bright blue borage flowers, wisteria, sprigs of lavender, rose petals, zucchini flowers, thyme sprigs and blossoms, basil or oregano flowers, small bright peppers, violets, geraniums, and fennel or celery fronds.

EXTRA-VIRGIN OLIVE OIL

The olive tree springs from the taproot of Mediterranean life. Over time, I've heard of olive oil being used for everything from stretch marks to kidney stones to coughs. After caring for a grove, it's impossible not to think of olive oil as a holy substance. The biblical references to anointing the body with oil had to have meant olive oil. Who first squeezed those bitter drupes and discovered the oil? She's our missing goddess or saint! She found the soul of the Mediterranean diet.

How to describe the distinct, polyphonic, greeny, assertive, fresh, piquant, sublime taste of just-pressed extra-virgin olive oil? Every year at harvest, I marvel at the punch it delivers to everything I cook. At this stage, just-pressed oil is bursting with health-improving properties, as well as that indescribable taste. Your cooking skills quadruple when you cook with the freshest oil available. Tuscans use great olive oil every day. When I first arrived in Tuscany, I was surprised to see Don Ferruccio, a local priest, eating an orange that he doused in olive oil and salt. That was a defining moment for me; I realized in one bite what I'd missed.

Since *everything in moderation* could be the Tuscan motto, cooks use just enough olive oil. Salads remain crisp when just glistened with olive oil, and maybe, not always, a hint of vinegar or lemon juice, then a judicious sprinkling of salt. On meats, the bottle tips farther: a liberal swathing of the steak or roast produces rich juices.

Finding an excellent oil takes a little work. Be sure to look at the expiration date *and* the harvest date. Naturally, the further away the expiration date, the better. Well-stored oil lasts a long time, just slowly losing its pep over time. The oil you're reaching for at the grocery store might have sat for months in the light. Even a week in a sunny window and it's lost. A dark bottle protects better than a clear one—but you can't see what you're buying. If the bottle has the DOP (Denominazione di Origine Protetta) sticker—bright blue and yellow—that's an Italian government guarantee that the oil is from the area stated on the bottle and that it was bottled there. The IGP (Indicazione Geografica Protetta) is a slightly less comprehensive guarantee, but if you see it, you know that the oil is from a specific region. Italy being Italy, however, means that some top oil makers don't bother with the sticker because the process of getting approval is baroque and delays sales while the oil is fresh. More and more growers who take pride in their oil are stating on the label where their olives were grown and where they were bottled.

Also look on the label for a location. If it says "Product of Italy," or product of any-where, that probably means it's a blend of olive oils (from who knows where) that was bottled in Italy. I consider this an iffy situation. Oils labeled like this may be good. You can't know unless you try them.

"Extra-virgin" means that the acid content is less than 0.8 percent. Never buy any oil that is *not* extra virgin unless you need to oil hinges. The designation "light" or—ugh—"lite" means absolutely nothing, and "cold-pressed" means less than it used to. The machinery began to change over a decade ago and all high-quality olive oil is pressed without the use of heat.

Many inexpensive extra-virgin oils sold in American discount stores are blends of oils that did not sell in their first year. If an extra-virgin olive oil from Italy is cheap, I'm 99 percent sure that something is amiss. When you know that a tree in Tuscany pro-duces one liter, you understand that first-quality oil has to be expensive. So, look with care at the olive oils in grocery stores, as well as in the fine cookware shops. Many verge on expiring and the labels are rife with misleading information! All you can read on the subject will arm you against buying a dreary product—an unholy mix or stale olive oil, or a lower quality older oil, even if it is "extra-virgin." For the price of a dinner out, you can buy enough fine oil to last for months and push your cooking from excellent to sublime!

After all these *caveat emptors*, there's the trial and error of finding the wonderful, enhancing oil you'll want for your house. Use it with confidence. Normal cooking heat does not destroy the qualities of good oil. Tuscans use it for frying, though you never read that in American cookbooks. Frequently they use olive oil instead of butter in baking. Fresh Tuscan oil has a kick, a tingly sensation, and a lively personality. With olive oil, you're not after the neutrality of other vegetable oils (or the chemical additives of refining processes); you want that clean life and spice and vibrancy that add so much depth to your food. If you travel to Italy in the fall, visit a *molino* and taste the just-pressed oil—a revelation. From massaging the newborn's umbilical cord to anointing the body for the shroud, olive oil always has been *the* essential ingredi-ent of Italian life.

ANTIPASTI

People obviously and thoroughly enjoy each other, especially gathering, preparing, and sharing food. Another plate or three or four, where's the bother? At a summer dinner, Marco looks down the row of plates and says, "It's good to have at least twenty at dinner," and he's right. Naturally, children and elders come to the table, too, and no one minds if the dog looks longingly at the bones. The host is grilling at the fireplace, guests arrive with bottles of wine, melons, and baskets of whatever their gardens are yielding at the moment. Friends help bring out large platters of *antipasti* to the laden table overlooking the valley. The ambience of the Tuscan table never feels like a dinner party but as if, somehow, *you've come home.*

—FROM *In Tuscany*

ANTIPASTI

BRUSCHETTE AND CROSTINI *41*

   ROASTED TOMATO *43*

   ARUGULA PESTO *43*

   GRILLED RED RADICCHIO *43*

   PEA AND SHALLOT *44*

   CANNELLINI BEAN AND SAGE *44*

   ROASTED GARLIC *46*

   PECORINO AND NUT *46*

   RED PEPPERS MELTED WITH BALSAMIC VINEGAR *47*

   ED'S CROSTINI NERI *47*

FRIED ZUCCHINI FLOWERS *49*

FRIED SAGE LEAVES *49*

FRIED ARTICHOKES *50*

WHEN-IN-ROME ARTICHOKES *53*

CAPONATA *54*

OLIVES, THREE WAYS *55*

   QUITE SPICY OLIVES *55*

   BAKED OLIVES WITH CITRUS PEEL AND GARLIC *55*

   OLIVE ALL'ASCOLANA *56*

FARRO SALAD *57*

CAPRESE *58*

ROLLED BRESAOLA *58*

PROSCIUTTO AND MELON *58*

FIORELLA'S RED PEPPER TART *59*

STAR OF THE SEA GRATINATO *60*

The antipasto course—welcome to the table! All menus in Tuscany offer an *antipasto misto*, mixed antipasto, and if friends are dining together, they're sure to say, "Shall we just order the *misto*?" Soon you find your plate crowded with *bruschette*, prosciutto and melon, a slice of frittata, *crostini*, various *salumi*, marinated artichokes, chunks of pecorino, grilled eggplant, and *bocconcini*, the delectable small balls of *mozzarella di bufala*—whatever the chef selects to lure you happily into dinner. Either informal or lavish, an antipasto course starts dinner with appeal and drama.

For an outdoor lunch, I rely on extensive antipasti and often follow them just with a pasta and dessert. Crowded platters circling the table create a festive mood and everyone finds something to want. Even a quiet dinner at home in Tuscany starts with one or two antipasti, maybe only some baked olives and a few *crostini* with spicy tomato sauce.

From the recipes that follow, put together elaborate antipasto platters, or choose one special recipe to serve as your overture, perhaps farro salad cupped in a red radicchio leaf or seafood *gratinato,* or a mound of crisp, fried zucchini flowers.

From this clarion call, you move happily onward to the feast.

When assembling antipasti, I pay as much attention to texture and color as I do to a variety of tastes. Hunting and gathering provide much of the fun. I enjoy the assembly: raid the pantry, open a few jars, and unwrap a choice pecorino. These are some easy choices—no need for a recipe:

ROASTED BELL PEPPERS

ARTICHOKE HEARTS WITH
EXTRA-VIRGIN OLIVE OIL

FENNEL SLICES SPRINKLED WITH
FENNEL SEEDS AND EXTRA-VIRGIN
OLIVE OIL

BREADSTICKS WRAPPED IN
PROSCIUTTO

GRILLED SHRIMP AND MELON CUBES
ON TOOTHPICKS

HALVED FIGS

SMALL CHUNKS OF PECORINO, GRANA
PADANO, OR PARMIGIANO-REGGIANO

BIG CAPERS, STEMS ON

TARALLI (CRUSTY BREAD TWISTS
AVAILABLE IN ITALIAN SPECIALTY
MARKETS) FLAVORED WITH
PEPERONCINI OR FENNEL SEEDS

VARIOUS *SALUMI*

Bruschette and *crostini*, the heart and soul of the antipasto course, are more than grilled bread and "little crusts"; they're the beginning of the ritual and fact of eating together. At home or in any trattoria, they jump-start the meal, which then proceeds to *il primo*, the pasta, risotto, or soup course, then *il secondo*, the meat and vegetable course, then comes the sweet end to the rhythmic sequence, *dolce*.

Eating out with friends, we love to order *crostini caldi*, the warm ones, along with the room-temp *crostini* topped with goat cheese and herbs, or spicy tomato sauce, or melted fontina with a bit of black truffle. The platters circulate for so long that we could just move on to dessert and forget the other two courses waiting to be ordered. But here comes the platter again, and we slide a few more *crostini* onto our plates.

BRUSCHETTE AND CROSTINI

Maybe *bruschetta* tastes best in its simplest form: grilled, rustic bread abundantly doused with green, fresh extra-virgin olive oil and salt, perhaps a quick rub of garlic. Is this the greatest thing that can happen to a piece of bread? This paradigm *bruschetta* represents the essence of Tuscan food, food that usually provokes me to say, "How can something so *easy* be this good?" Quintessential as the basic *bruschetta* can be, it's still tempting to serve several other types of *bruschette* on the antipasto platter.

Crostini, the antipasti that appear at every party in Tuscany, and *bruschette* are both slices of bread with various toppings. The difference? *Bruschette* are larger, sliced from a regular, hearty loaf, while *crostini* are small rounds from a baguette-type loaf called a *stinco,* shinbone. *Bruschette* are always grilled or toasted; *crostini* usually are not, though *crostini caldi* are.

A typical platter of *crostini* includes several tempting choices. *Crostini neri*—topped with a "black" chicken liver spread—are, no question, the local favorite. If you dislike them, don't tell anyone! In restaurants, I like to find *crostini* with Gorgonzola and walnuts, with roasted garlic and grilled shrimp, or with oven-roasted tomatoes. All summer and into fall, platters of *bruschette* topped with fresh juicy tomatoes and basil make the rounds of the table, along with refreshing melon slices or figs with prosciutto. Winter's robust *bruschette* with black cabbage or puréed cannellini beans and sage are fun to prepare at the fireplace.

Each recipe serves 8 to 12, depending on the size of the bread you use and how generously you apply the toppings. Usually one portion of *bruschetta* or three to four *crostini* suffice. *Bruschette* and *crostini* are not reserved for antipasti—these recipes add their infinite variety to *pranzo,* lunch, and *merenda,* snack.

On the following pages are some of the best toppings, excellent for both *crostini* or the larger *bruschette.* Or even for crackers.

PREPARING BRUSCHETTE AND CROSTINI

For *bruschetta,* grill or broil substantial slices of rustic Tuscan bread, brush with extra-virgin olive oil, and sprinkle with salt. If you like, spear a clove of garlic with one side cut and rub the cut side across the bread before adding the olive oil. I usually cut the *bruschette* in half unless it's being served at the table, because if you're standing up, big *bruschette* can be unruly. For *crostini,* cut a long skinny loaf into slices about ⅓ inch thick. Toast them or not, depending on the topping.

ROASTED TOMATO

This is your ace. In summer, the trio of chopped, luscious tomatoes, olive oil, and fresh herbs sings the national anthem.

In winter, canned or boxed tomatoes attain a new depth of flavor during a long nap in the oven. The plump little darlings garnish a roast or, chopped, wake up a last-minute risotto or frittata.

If you want heat, scatter a tablespoon of *peperoncini*, red pepper flakes, over the tomatoes while cooking.

60 OR SO CHERRY TOMATOES, HALVED, STEM ENDS TRIMMED; OR 25 MEDIUM TOMATOES, QUARTERED; OR 3 28-OUNCE CANS SAN MARZANO PLUM TOMATOES, DRAINED, CUT INTO QUARTERS

½ CUP EXTRA-VIRGIN OLIVE OIL

3 TABLESPOONS MINCED FRESH ROSEMARY OR 1½ TABLESPOONS DRIED

3 TABLESPOONS FRESH THYME LEAVES OR 1½ TABLESPOONS DRIED

3 TABLESPOONS FRESH OREGANO LEAVES OR 1½ TABLESPOONS DRIED

5 GARLIC CLOVES, CHOPPED

SALT AND PEPPER TO TASTE

PREPARED *BRUSCHETTE* OR *CROSTINI*

Preheat the oven to 200°F.

Arrange the tomatoes cut side up on a parchment-lined 12 x 16-inch sheet pan. Drizzle the olive oil over them, scatter the herbs and garlic, and season with salt and pepper. Bake for 2 hours, turning the tomatoes once.

Coarsely chop the tomatoes for *bruschette,* or simply press a tomato onto each *crostino.*

Leftover tomatoes can be packed into jars, topped with olive oil, and stored in the fridge for a week.

ARUGULA PESTO

 1 BUNCH OF YOUNG ARUGULA, STEMS REMOVED
½ TEASPOON SALT
½ TEASPOON PEPPER
 2 GARLIC CLOVES
¼ CUP PINE NUTS
 3 TABLESPOONS EXTRA-VIRGIN OLIVE OIL
½ CUP (2 OUNCES) GRATED PARMIGIANO-REGGIANO
   PREPARED *CROSTINI*

In a food processor or mortar, combine the arugula, salt, pepper, garlic, and pine nuts. Blend well, and then slowly incorporate enough olive oil to make a thick paste. Pulse or stir in the Parmigiano. Spread on bread.

Rucola, arugula, is satisfying to grow, though you must sow the seeds weekly. It sprouts quickly and the young peppery leaves are best. Savor immediately because arugula bolts while you look the other way. The wilder cousin is *rughetta*, which has an intense bite of intriguing bitterness.

GRILLED RED RADICCHIO

    1 HEAD OF RED RADICCHIO
2 TO 3 TABLESPOONS EXTRA-VIRGIN OLIVE OIL
    3 SLICES PROSCIUTTO, CUT INTO SLIVERS
   ¼ TEASPOON SALT
   ¼ TEASPOON PEPPER
   ½ TEASPOON FENNEL SEEDS, CRUSHED
     PREPARED *BRUSCHETTE* OR *CROSTINI*

Cut the radicchio head in two and put each half face down on a medium-heated grill. (You can, instead, use a 16-inch stovetop grill pan.) Let the radicchio slightly brown, 3 or 4 minutes, then turn the halves over with tongs and grill the other side for 2 or 3 minutes.

When cool, chop the radicchio and place it in a medium bowl. Douse with 2 tablespoons of the olive oil, and stir in the prosciutto, seasonings, and fennel seeds. Add a little more olive oil if it looks dry. Pile on the prepared bread.

Small cubes of fontina or pecorino can be used with, or instead of, the prosciutto. This can be served, too, as a salad in whole leaves of the radicchio, which form pretty red cups.

PEA *and* SHALLOT

Since pea season is brief, I like to buy a bushel and corral someone to help me shell them. I freeze them in two-cup portions.

4 SHALLOTS, MINCED
2 CUPS PEAS, SHELLED
2 TABLESPOONS EXTRA-VIRGIN OLIVE OIL
3 TABLESPOONS CHOPPED MINT
2 TABLESPOONS MASCARPONE
¼ TEASPOON SALT
¼ TEASPOON PEPPER
PREPARED *BRUSCHETTE* OR *CROSTINI*

In a medium pan over medium heat, mix the shallots with the peas, and sauté in the olive oil until the peas are barely done and the shallots are wilted, about 4 minutes. Stir in the mint, mascarpone, salt, and pepper. Chop coarsely in a food processor or by hand, and spoon onto the bread.

CANNELLINI BEAN *and* SAGE

When you buy the beans, be sure to check the sell-by date. The longer away it is, the better. If the beans are older, the soaking or cooking time will be longer. Watch and taste—if they turn mushy, there's nothing to do but purée them with some stock for a lovely soup. Before starting, read the note on cooking beans and chickpeas on page 24.

1 POUND DRIED CANNELLINI BEANS, COOKED (PAGE 24)
3 TABLESPOONS EXTRA-VIRGIN OLIVE OIL
8 TO 10 FRESH SAGE LEAVES, CHOPPED, PLUS MORE WHOLE LEAVES FOR GARNISH
1 GARLIC CLOVE, MINCED
1 TEASPOON SALT
½ TEASPOON PEPPER
PREPARED *BRUSCHETTE* OR *CROSTINI*

By hand or in a food processor, lightly chop the beans, and add the olive oil, sage, garlic, salt, and pepper, being careful not to turn the mixture into a purée. Spread on the bread and garnish each with whole sage leaves.

ROASTED GARLIC

8 WHOLE HEADS OF GARLIC
½ CUP EXTRA-VIRGIN OLIVE OIL
SALT TO TASTE
PREPARED *BRUSCHETTE* OR *CROSTINI*

Fresh garlic doesn't have the bitter taste older garlic gets, mainly from the sprout in the center. Remove the sprout by slicing the clove in half and lifting out the green center with the tip of a knife. The heads of garlic should be dense, and the "paper" quite white.

As a variation on this recipe, toast and chop ½ cup of walnuts, add them to the garlic purée, and spread on *crostini*. As *bruschetta*, float it in your soup bowl, the way *contadini*, farmers, have done for centuries.

Preheat the oven to 400°F.

Gently remove most of the papery outer skin of the garlic bulb and slice off the very top of the head, exposing the cloves. Place each head on a square of aluminum foil. Pour over the cut surface a tablespoon of olive oil, sprinkle with salt, and close the foil into tight bundles. Place the bundles in a small ovenproof dish.

Roast for 30 to 40 minutes, checking with fork tines after the first 30 minutes. When the tines easily pierce the garlic, it's done. The cloves will lightly brown.

Let the garlic cool until ready to handle. Squeeze out the garlic head with the heel of your hand, or take a paring knife and carefully dig out the cloves from the top. Or, and this seems best to me, separate the cloves gently and let your guests squeeze out the garlic directly onto their bread.

PECORINO *and* NUT

8 SLICES PECORINO OR FONTINA
¼ CUP WALNUTS, CHOPPED
PREPARED *BRUSCHETTE* OR *CROSTINI*

Beneath the cheese and nuts, you can slip thinly sliced salami or prosciutto.

Preheat the broiler.

Place a slice of pecorino and some walnuts on each piece of bread. Run under the broiler for a couple of minutes until slightly melted.

RED PEPPERS MELTED *with* BALSAMIC VINEGAR

- 3 RED BELL PEPPERS, SEEDED AND THINLY SLICED
- ½ CUP BLACK OLIVES, PITTED
- 3 TABLESPOONS EXTRA-VIRGIN OLIVE OIL, OR MORE IF NEEDED
- ¼ CUP BALSAMIC VINEGAR, OR MORE IF NEEDED
- ¼ TEASPOON SALT
- ¼ TEASPOON PEPPER
- PREPARED *BRUSCHETTE* OR *CROSTINI*

In a large skillet on lowest heat, cook the peppers and olives, uncovered, with the olive oil and balsamic vinegar until the peppers are soft, about 40 minutes. Stir occasionally; the peppers should almost "melt." Add more olive oil and balsamic vinegar if they look dry. Season with salt and pepper. Spoon peppers onto bread and serve warm.

Melted red peppers top *bruschette* perfectly, but just solo they're a colorful marker on the antipasto platter. Leftovers are great on polenta with sausages. With cheese and grilled eggplant, savory sandwiches come together quickly. If you scatter a minced dried hot red pepper, seeds removed, over the bell peppers while they're cooking, you'll have a spicy spread.

Ed's CROSTINI NERI

- ½ CUP *SOFFRITTO* (PAGE 20)
- 3 ANCHOVY FILLETS
- 2 TABLESPOONS EXTRA-VIRGIN OLIVE OIL
- 1 POUND CHICKEN LIVERS, TRIMMED
- ½ TEASPOON SALT
- ½ TEASPOON PEPPER
- ½ CUP RED WINE
- 2 TABLESPOONS BALSAMIC VINEGAR
- 1 TABLESPOON CAPERS, DRAINED
- PREPARED *CROSTINI*

In a medium skillet over medium-low heat, sauté the *soffritto* and anchovies in the olive oil until the anchovies begin to dissolve, about 3 minutes. Wash and pat dry the chicken livers, season with salt and pepper, and add them to the pan, browning on all sides. Press with a wooden spoon from time to time. After 8 to 10 minutes, add the wine and vinegar. Raise the heat to medium and cook, uncovered, until most of the liquid has evaporated, about 10 minutes. In the last few minutes of cooking, stir in the capers. For a finer texture, chop the mixture briefly in a food processor. Serve either warm or at room temperature on *crostini*.

Crostini neri—black *crostini*. Chopped liver? No way. This is *the* Tuscan recipe, the universal favorite, starring at every feast. I'm always astounded at how quickly they disappear, no matter how many trays are passed around.

FRIED ZUCCHINI FLOWERS

    2   CUPS PEANUT OR SUNFLOWER OIL, FOR FRYING
   24   MALE ZUCCHINI FLOWERS, UNWASHED

BATTER FOR FRYING
    1   CUP ALL-PURPOSE FLOUR
   ½   TEASPOON SALT
    1   CUP BEER

        COARSE SALT TO TASTE

In a medium skillet, heat the oil to 350°F.

If the blossoms are moist, pat them dry with a paper towel. Gently pry open each flower and break off the yellow stamen, or use tweezers to snip it out.

To prepare the batter, in a medium bowl, mix the flour, salt, and beer, and let this rest for 20 minutes. Break up any lumps with a fork. Quickly dip each flower into the batter, coating it all over.

Slip the flowers into the oil. Flip once. Fry in batches until tawny and crispy, about 2 minutes. Remove them with the spatula or tongs, and drain quickly on paper towels. Serve immediately, with a sprinkling of salt.

When this is good it's very, very good, and when it's limp it's a disaster. To avoid the latter, the oil must maintain a steady temperature. Choose a fresh bunch of flowers; if they're slightly droopy, don't bother. The male plants do not develop into zucchini—they only flower. If you're growing zucchini, pick tiny ones with the flowers still attached. Cut these zucchini and flowers down the center and fry them with male flowers. Young squash blossoms work equally well.

FRIED SAGE LEAVES

SERVES 8

        BATTER FOR FRYING (ABOVE; USE ½ RECIPE)
    1   CUP PEANUT OR SUNFLOWER OIL, FOR FRYING
   32   SAGE LEAVES

Prepare the batter and let it rest for 20 minutes.

In a medium skillet, heat the oil to 350°F.

Wash the sage if necessary, and pat it with a dishtowel to dry completely. Dip the sage leaves into the batter and drop them into the oil for 1 to 2 minutes (depending on the thickness of the leaves), or until the leaves are crisp. Drain on paper towels and serve immediately.

Too often, sage is associated with that green dust that comes in little jars and makes you sneeze. Fresh sage has an assertive punch. Fry these as a garnish for meat or serve them along with fried zucchini flowers and drinks.

FRIED ARTICHOKES

As a Southerner, to me the words "deep fried" are an enchanting combination. We never met an artichoke, when I was growing up, except the kind that was marinated in a jar. Still, *carciofi fritti* seem like soul food.

At the Thursday market in season, vendors, many of whom have driven their trucks all night from Puglia, sell five sizes of artichokes. For stuffing with bread, herbs, and tomatoes, I buy the largest ones. For frying, the smallest, purple-tinged *violetti* or *morellini* are best. Tiny *violetti*, sliced raw and dressed, make an astringent crunchy salad, which exemplifies the Tuscan preference for bitter tastes.

For these fried beauties, remember that the stem is as tasty as the heart. Sometimes four or five inches long, the stems can be peeled with a vegetable peeler. Cut each artichoke in half, leaving the stem attached. If they're small enough, fry them like this. If not, slice each in half again, paring off any choke. Be sure to remove all tough outer leaves.

Matching wine with artichokes is daunting, but we've tried fried artichokes with Friulano, formerly called Tocai, the darling of the province of Friuli-Venezia-Giulia. The usual suggestion, however, is a Gewürztraminer.

SERVES 4

BATTER FOR FRYING (PAGE 49)
2 CUPS PEANUT OR SUNFLOWER OIL, FOR FRYING
15 VERY SMALL ARTICHOKES
COARSE SALT TO TASTE
LEMON WEDGES, FOR GARNISH

Prepare the batter and let it rest for 20 minutes.

In a medium skillet, heat the oil to 350°F.

Strip all tough outer leaves from the artichokes and cut away the top third. Trim off any sharp tips from the lower leaves. Halve or quarter the artichokes.

Dip the artichokes in the batter, and then slide them into the oil. Fry the artichokes in batches until crisp and browned, about 4 minutes, depending on size. When done, remove them to paper towels to drain, salt immediately, then pile them on a board and pass with wedges of lemon.

WHEN-IN-ROME ARTICHOKES

SERVES 8

- 8 LARGE ARTICHOKES, TOPS AND BOTTOMS TRIMMED, SHARP POINTS OF LEAVES CUT AWAY, ALL ROUGH LEAVES REMOVED
- 3 GARLIC CLOVES, MINCED
  JUICE AND ZEST OF 2 LEMONS
- ½ CUP EXTRA-VIRGIN OLIVE OIL
- 1 TEASPOON SALT
- ½ TEASPOON PEPPER
- 1 HANDFUL OF FLAT-LEAF PARSLEY, CHOPPED
- 4 SLICES RUSTIC BREAD, CUT INTO 1-INCH SQUARES AND TOASTED
- 4 TOMATOES, CUT INTO LARGE DICE

Bring a large steamer of water to a boil, and cook the artichokes, partially covered, for about 20 minutes. Test for doneness by piercing the bottom with a fork, or by pulling a petal, which should only slightly resist. It should be yielding but not soft. Cool the artichokes, and then gently pry apart the leaves, exposing the choke. Pull out the tuft, and scrape the heart clean with a spoon.

Mix the garlic, lemon juice, zest, olive oil, seasonings, and parsley in a glass jar and shake it well.

In a medium bowl, toss the bread and tomatoes with 2 tablespoons of the lemon and olive oil mixture. With your fingers, spread open each artichoke and fill the cavities with the bread and tomato mixture. Insert bread and tomatoes inside the leaves so that the artichoke is studded all around. Arrange the little beauties on plates, and douse each one all over with the remaining lemon and olive oil mixture.

Italians adore celebrating seasonal food. For over sixty years, artichokes have been the focus of the Sagra del Carciofo Romanesco in Ladispoli. The *romanesco* is the BIG artichoke. "Sagra" denotes a festival—in autumn it'll be *zucca*, *castagna*, *polenta*, *cinghiale* (pumpkin, chestnut, polenta, boar); in summer, *lumache*, *ciliegie*, *oca* (snails, cherries, goose)—whatever the region boasts at the moment. The *sagra* signs lure you to follow your nose. The festivals are lively; the food, extraordinary. I'd like to go to Ladispoli for the April *sagra* because we're always looking for new ways to serve artichokes.

I've made this constructed artichoke a thousand times. Its talents take it to center stage as antipasto, first course, or the main attraction at lunch. It's fun to assemble these with a child because it's like decorating the Christmas tree.

CAPONATA

SERVES 15 TO 20

The Sicilian version of *caponata* that I tasted in Siracusa was more flavorful than mine. Why? The concentrated tomato *estratto* (tomato paste made from sun-dried tomatoes) available in Sicily, a freer hand with seasoning, and the umami lent by the anchovies. I came home and gave my *caponata* a boost.

This is one of those perfect antipasti to have on hand for guests. Place a bowl of *caponata* amid crackers and crudités and serve it forth. At lunch, a couple of tablespoons of this turns a plain ham or tomato sandwich into something special, and it's also a great pasta sauce—just toss with penne. Like many tomato-based recipes, *caponata* is best if made a day ahead. It will keep in the fridge for a week.

2   MEDIUM EGGPLANTS, SLICED ½ INCH THICK
6   TABLESPOONS EXTRA-VIRGIN OLIVE OIL
1   LARGE YELLOW ONION, FINELY CHOPPED
4   GARLIC CLOVES, MINCED
6   SUN-DRIED TOMATOES, SOAKED FOR 1 HOUR IN 2 TABLESPOONS EXTRA-VIRGIN OLIVE OIL, THEN CHOPPED
½   CUP TOMATO PASTE
1   CUP TOMATO SAUCE (PAGE 21)
4   ANCHOVY FILLETS, CHOPPED
2   TABLESPOONS SALTED CAPERS, RINSED AND LEFT WHOLE
1   HANDFUL OF FLAT-LEAF PARSLEY, CHOPPED
½   CUP PITTED GREEN OLIVES, COARSELY CHOPPED
½   CUP PITTED BLACK OLIVES, COARSELY CHOPPED
1   TABLESPOON FRESH OREGANO LEAVES OR 1½ TEASPOONS DRIED
1   TEASPOON SALT
1   TEASPOON PEPPER
¼   TEASPOON PEPERONCINI (RED PEPPER FLAKES), OR MORE TO TASTE

Preheat the oven to 400°F.

Place the eggplant slices on a parchment-lined sheet pan, drizzle with 4 tablespoons of the olive oil, and bake for 15 to 20 minutes, until softened and slightly browned.

In a 12-inch skillet over medium heat, sauté the onion in the remaining 2 tablespoons olive oil until translucent, about 5 minutes. Add the garlic and sauté for another minute. Cut the eggplant slices into small cubes, add to the onion, and cook to blend, about 3 minutes. The onion and eggplant are now ready for their jolt of color. Add the sun-dried tomatoes and their oil, tomato paste, and tomato sauce to the eggplant mixture. Stir well and toss to combine. Turn the heat to low and add the anchovies, capers, parsley, and olives. Stir in the oregano, salt, pepper, and red pepper flakes. Let the *caponata* warm through. Serve it right away, or if you chill it for later, let it come to room temperature before serving.

OLIVES, THREE WAYS

Olives are fine on their own, but here are three twists on the usual—one spicy, one lemony, and one stuffed and fried. Try all three when there are guests. With this olive threesome, I like breadsticks wrapped with prosciutto, chunks of aged pecorino, *finocchiona* (fennel-scented salami), and dry Cinzano on the rocks.

QUITE SPICY OLIVES

SERVES 10 TO 15

- 2 SMALL HOT PEPPERS (1 RED AND 1 GREEN), SEEDED AND MINCED, OR 1 TABLESPOON PEPERONCINI (RED PEPPER FLAKES)
- 1 MEDIUM YELLOW ONION, MINCED
- 2 TABLESPOONS EXTRA-VIRGIN OLIVE OIL
- 2 CUPS LARGE GREEN OLIVES
- 1 TEASPOON SALT
- 2 TABLESPOONS LEMON JUICE

If the olives are pitted, you can fill each one with a whole roasted almond.

In a small skillet over medium-low heat, cook the hot peppers or red pepper flakes with the onion in 1 tablespoon of the olive oil for 3 or 4 minutes, or until the onion is translucent and on the verge of browning. Mix in the olives, moisten with the remaining tablespoon of olive oil, and add the salt and lemon juice. Transfer the olives to a covered glass dish and let them rest in the fridge overnight.

BAKED OLIVES *with* CITRUS PEEL *and* GARLIC

SERVES 10 TO 15

- PEEL OF 1 LEMON
- PEEL OF 1 ORANGE
- 2 CUPS MIXED GREEN AND BLACK OLIVES
- 6 GARLIC CLOVES, QUARTERED
- 1 TABLESPOON RED WINE
- ½ TEASPOON FRESH OREGANO LEAVES OR ¼ TEASPOON DRIED
- 3 TABLESPOONS EXTRA-VIRGIN OLIVE OIL

Just one of these can set you dreaming of Capri or Ravello.

Preheat the oven to 350°F.

After removing the citrus peel in thin strips, cut the strips into pieces an inch or so long. Mix everything in a small, open earthenware baking dish. Bake for 20 minutes, and serve in the same dish.

OLIVE *all'*ASCOLANA

SERVES 8

In the Marche region, the 50,000 *ascolani*, the people who live in Ascoli Piceno, dwell around one of the most beautiful piazzas in Italy, the Piazza del Popolo. At cafés in early evening, everyone is sipping prosecco and nibbling stuffed fried olives, a local treat famous all over Italy. Traditionally filled with ground meats, the olives also show an affinity for chopped salami. The olive of choice is their local one, the quite large and green Ascolano Tenera.

Use any large, pitted green olives. For an alternative filling: with a pastry tube, try piping in a mix of roasted garlic, anchovy, and lemon zest.

- 1 CUP PEANUT OIL OR SUNFLOWER OIL, FOR FRYING
- ½ CUP ALL-PURPOSE FLOUR
- 2 EGGS, BEATEN
- ¾ CUP FRESH BREADCRUMBS
- ¼ TEASPOON PEPPER
- 24 LARGE GREEN OLIVES, PITTED
- ¼ POUND SLICED ITALIAN SALAMI, PREFERABLY FINOCCHIONA, FINELY CHOPPED

In a medium skillet, heat the oil to 350°F.

Place the flour, beaten egg, and breadcrumbs in three separate small bowls. Season the flour with pepper. Stuff the olives with the salami, and then roll them in the flour, then the egg, and finally the breadcrumbs. Fry until golden, turning when needed, about 2 minutes. Drain on paper towels and serve immediately.

FARRO SALAD

SERVES 10, WITH LEFTOVERS

- 3 CUPS FARRO
- 1 ONION, QUARTERED
- 4 CELERY STALKS, 3 FINELY CHOPPED AND 1 LEFT WHOLE
- 3 CARROTS, 2 MINCED AND 1 LEFT WHOLE
- 4 TOMATOES, SEEDED AND CHOPPED
- ½ CUP PITTED GREEN OLIVES, CUT IN HALF
- 2 SHALLOTS, MINCED
- 3 GARLIC CLOVES, MINCED
- ½ CUP EXTRA-VIRGIN OLIVE OIL
- 1 HANDFUL OF BASIL LEAVES, TORN
- 1 BUNCH OF FLAT-LEAF PARSLEY, CHOPPED
  JUICE AND ZEST OF 1 LEMON
- ¼ CUP PINE NUTS, TOASTED
  SALT AND PEPPER TO TASTE

Pour the farro into a 6-quart pot of cold water. Add the onion, the whole celery stalk, and the whole carrot. Bring to a boil, immediately lower to a simmer, partially cover, and cook, stirring now and then, until the farro is done, usually in under an hour. Start tasting after 45 minutes. It should have the same texture as rice. If overcooked, it turns goopy.

While the farro is cooking, mix all the other ingredients in a medium bowl. Drain the farro, and return it to the pot. Discard the cooked vegetables. Add the vegetable mixture to the farro, and toss well. Correct seasonings and serve.

A scoop of farro salad, tucked into a red radicchio leaf, adds texture to an antipasto platter. Leftover farro keeps in the fridge for three to four days and is handy for wraps. Farro (the grain *Triticum dicoccum*) is no longer difficult to locate. Spelt it's not, though you do see that identification. Farro is an ancient grain that almost fell out of use for centuries and has been restored as a viable crop. Nutty and chewy, it tastes like a cross between brown rice and wheat berries—but, really, it just tastes like farro.

If you use husked *farro perlato*, pearled farro, it will cook in 20 minutes. Look for whole-grain or semi-pearled farro. If the label doesn't say, monitor the cooking time. Farro salad is one of a triumvirate I usually serve at pool and bocce parties, along with a green salad and a fennel and orange salad.

CAPRESE

SERVES 8

The quality of the mozzarella means everything in this classic summer salad. Instead of the brick-shaped mozzarella, use the delicate and rich *mozzarella di bufala*, the water buffalo cheese that comes suspended in bags of liquid to keep it moist.

20	SLICES TOMATO, ABOUT 5 MEDIUM
20	SLICES *MOZZARELLA DI BUFALA*
5	TABLESPOONS EXTRA-VIRGIN OLIVE OIL
½	TEASPOON SALT
½	TEASPOON PEPPER
20	BASIL LEAVES, TORN

Alternate the tomato and mozzarella slices in concentric circles, drizzle the olive oil all over them, season with salt and pepper, and scatter the basil leaves on top.

ROLLED BRESAOLA

SERVES 8

Robiola, from Lombardia and Piemonte, is usually made from cow milk, but Robiola di Roccaverano is almost all goat milk. Try them both. If no Robiola is available, use cream cheese, which will be fine once it's dressed up with herbs.

4	OUNCES ROBIOLA
	A BIG HANDFUL OF ARUGULA, CHOPPED
2	TEASPOONS FRESH THYME LEAVES
2	TEASPOONS CHOPPED FRESH CHIVES
	PEPPER TO TASTE
16	SLICES BRESAOLA (DRIED SALTED BEEF)

In a small bowl, combine the Robiola with the arugula, thyme, chives, and pepper. Spread the Robiola on the slices of bresaola and roll up. Place on a platter seam side down.

PROSCIUTTO *and* MELON

Simple and classic, *prosciutto e melone* starts off many a summer dinner all over Italy. Cut a melon into 8 crescents, remove the seeds and rind, and arrange on a plate with the thinnest slices of prosciutto. Garnish with mint or lemon balm leaves. *Basta!* Enough!

Fiorella's RED PEPPER TART

SERVES 8

1	YELLOW ONION, THINLY SLICED
3	TABLESPOONS EXTRA-VIRGIN OLIVE OIL
3	MEDIUM ZUCCHINI, THINLY SLICED
1	10-INCH FLAKY PASTRY PIECRUST (PAGE 194; MADE WITHOUT SUGAR)
3	EGGS
½	CUP (2 OUNCES) GRATED PARMIGIANO-REGGIANO
½	TEASPOON SALT
½	TEASPOON PEPPER
1	RED BELL PEPPER, CUT INTO SLIVERS

Fiorella makes everything from scratch, or so I thought. When she brought out this tart one summer night, she said it was "made in an instant." Later, she told me that for this only, she uses a purchased piecrust. When it emerges from the oven, the tart is puffed and golden, so rush it to the table.

Preheat the oven to 375°F.

In a medium skillet, sauté the onion in 2 tablespoons of the olive oil until translucent, about 3 minutes, over medium heat, then add the zucchini and let them cook together for 3 or 4 minutes more, until they are barely tender. Arrange the sautéed vegetables in the piecrust.

Break the eggs into a small bowl and whisk with the cheese and seasonings. Pour this over the onion and zucchini. Swab out the bowl, and toss the bell pepper in the remaining tablespoon of olive oil. Arrange the slices in a spoke pattern, pressing them down into the eggs a little. Bake for 30 minutes, until the center has domed and the pastry is flaky and browned. Serve immediately.

STAR *of the* SEA GRATINATO

SERVES 8

Redolent of beach cafés with a salty breeze, this shrimp and mussel *gratinato* stars as a solo antipasto or as a tasty first course. Before you begin, soak the saffron to yield the most flavor from this most expensive of seasonings. The sauce is optional, but Ed recommends a spoon or so for the intense golden taste. With this dish, Ed pours Venica & Venica, Collio DOC Traminer Aromatico.

- 3 SHALLOTS, MINCED
- 1¼ POUNDS WILD-CAUGHT MEDIUM SHRIMP, PEELED AND CLEANED
- 6 TABLESPOONS EXTRA-VIRGIN OLIVE OIL
- ¾ TEASPOON SALT
- ¼ TEASPOON PEPPER, PLUS ADDITIONAL TO TASTE
- 2 POUNDS MUSSELS, WASHED AND CLEANED WITH A BRUSH
- ¼ CUP COARSE FRESH BREADCRUMBS, TOASTED
- ¼ CUP (1 OUNCE) GRATED PARMIGIANO-REGGIANO
- ¼ CUP CHOPPED FLAT-LEAF PARSLEY
- 1 TEASPOON FRESH THYME OR ½ TEASPOON DRIED PINCH OF PEPERONCINI (RED PEPPER FLAKES)

FOR THE SAUCE

- PAN LIQUIDS FROM SHRIMP AND MUSSELS
- ¼ CUP WHITE WINE
- ½ CUP HEAVY CREAM
- ¼ TEASPOON SALT, PLUS ADDITIONAL TO TASTE
- 4 TO 5 SAFFRON THREADS

Soak the saffron threads in 2 tablespoons of tepid water for 1 hour.

Preheat the oven to 400°F.

In a large skillet over medium heat, sauté the shallots and shrimp in 2 tablespoons of olive oil until the shallots are translucent and the shrimp just start to turn pink, about 2 minutes. Season with ½ teaspoon of salt and the pepper. Remove to a large bowl. Add 2 more tablespoons of olive oil to the pan and raise the heat to medium high as you add the mussels. The heat causes the shells to open. Discard any that do not.

Leaving the liquid in the skillet, remove the mussels to a bowl with a slotted spoon and extract them from their shells. Mix them and any liquid from the mussels with the shrimp. Toss the seafood with the remaining 2 tablespoons olive oil. Mix in the breadcrumbs, Parmigiano, parsley, thyme, the remaining salt, and the red pepper flakes. Transfer to ½-cup buttered ramekins or scallop shells. Bake for 10 minutes.

Meanwhile, prepare the sauce. Bring the reserved pan liquids and wine to a boil and reduce by a third, about 5 minutes. Reduce the heat to low, and add the cream, salt, saffron, and saffron water. Continue to cook, stirring, for 3 to 4 minutes. Taste to see if a little more salt should be added. Serve the ramekins and pass the saffron sauce.

SAFFRON THREADS

Eight years ago, a friend of ours, Marco Bennati, started cultivating lavender crocuses (*Crocus sativus*) just outside Cortona, on a plot about the size of a football field. Every October, from three *quintale*, 660 pounds, of bulbs, he harvests a total of ½ pound of saffron—only the three threadlike stigmas are plucked out of the flower—which he then dries on baking sheets in the fireplace.

Saffron and other now-rare spices were used in earlier eras in Italian cooking. Hearing Marco describe the labor involved, it's easy to understand how the cultivation of saffron declined. He keeps beehives, too, and raises grapes and rare varieties of potatoes. As we walk over to the hives, he stays on the edge of the crocus field, swatting away bees that come near. Marco teaches at the agricultural school and passes on to the coming generation his passions, introducing them to artisans who are devoted to the revival of lost vegetable crops, planting vines in Etruscan patterns, ageing cheese in pits, making ricotta, and searching out old varieties of fruit trees.

When he gave me a few of his precious threads and some bulbs to plant, I asked him for his favorite saffron recipes. He laughed and said, "I must admit, I don't even like it." Luckily, he likes the crocuses and the whole growing process. And as he hands me a huge jar of honey, he tells me he's allergic to bee sting!

PRIMI

Maybe you've accepted an invitation to a Tuscan dinner, a long table under a grape pergola. The plates don't necessarily match and the wine is poured into tumblers. The table is laden with garden-fresh food, bread baked this morning, and wine that tastes of the Tuscan sun. This dinner never will be only dinner. Often it seems to me that a pact exists among the guests: everyone will shine; everyone will insure that others are cosseted, flattered, that they will laugh. The intimate society of diners creates this bond over and over. You are crowded together because the table seats only twenty and twenty-five have arrived. Friends play musical chairs throughout the evening so they get to visit with everyone. They may sing or play cards, get up to dance, even smoke those awful stubby cigars. The butcher may leap on the table and begin reciting Dante. Someone may fire a shotgun into the air. A dog will graze among the legs. Someone may shout out a proposal of marriage.

You never know what will happen in the course of a big night under the stars in Tuscany. You may even find yourself belting out "Unchained Melody" into a karaoke mike, as I did. When the ordinary leaps beyond ordinary, you follow. This table, at my neighbor's house, is set for the best life has to offer.

So, the long table. Shoes off. Fork poised. Pull up the extra chair for the stranger. Always, the garden. A basket by the back door. Let the butterflies and lizards and neighborhood cats have the run of the house. Windows open, heart and mind open. Fall into the round of giving melons, beans, jars of tomatoes. You are carried by something larger than yourself that is at the same time yourself. Salt the pasta water. And expect to be surprised. Always surprised.

—FROM *Every Day in Tuscany*

PRIMI

GIUSI'S RAGÙ *70*

TRENETTE WITH PESTO AND POTATOES *72*

IVAN'S PEAR AGNOLOTTI WITH GORGONZOLA AND WALNUTS *73*

SILVIA'S PASTA WITH DUCK SAUCE *76*

ORECCHIETTE WITH SHRIMP *77*

PICI WITH FRESH FAVA BEANS *78*

PANE E VINO'S PICI WITH BREADCRUMBS AND ANCHOVIES *80*

ANN CORNELISEN'S PASTA WITH ARUGULA AND PANCETTA *81*

PASTA SHELLS WITH SHRIMP AND THREE CHEESES *82*

SMOKY PASTA *83*

ANGRY PASTA *84*

SPAGHETTI WITH LEMON AND CRAB *85*

POTATO RAVIOLI WITH ZUCCHINI, SPECK, AND PECORINO *86*

LASAGNE WITH RAGÙ *88*

WILD MUSHROOM LASAGNE *89*

BAKED PASTA WITH SAUSAGE AND FOUR CHEESES *91*

SEMOLINA GNOCCHI *92*

GNOCCHI DI PATATE *93*

GARLIC SOUP *94*

YELLOW AND RED PEPPER SOUP *95*

PAPPA AL POMODORO *96*

MINESTRONE: BIG SOUP *97*

RIBOLLITA *98*

ONION SOUP IN THE AREZZO STYLE *99*

KALE, WHITE BEAN, AND SAUSAGE SOUP *100*

TWO TASTY RISOTTOS *101*

   SHRIMP RISOTTO *102*

   RISOTTO PRIMAVERA *103*

RISOTTO SALTATO *104*

PIZZA *105*

   IVAN'S PIZZA MARGHERITA *106*

   PIZZA WITH CARAMELIZED ONION AND SAUSAGE *107*

In Italy, there are as many pastas as paintings of the Virgin Mary. If you haven't lived among the Italians, it's hard to comprehend just what pasta means. What other food can be ethereal or earthy, plain or complex, saucy or dry, lusty or reserved, trendy or traditional, rugged or silky? Beyond the many-splendored versatility, pasta means more, much more. Pasta is a birthright. "I have eaten pasta every day of my life," Aurora tells me. At lunch, road workmen crowd into the *trattoria* and wolf down bowls of plain spaghetti doused with oil, lots of pepper, and a handful of Parmigiano. Italians *travel* with their favorite pastas so if, heaven forbid, they're stranded in some unenlightened place, they can at least put on a pot to boil. The six-month-old already is slurping soup with tiny pasta stars swimming in the broth. When our neighbor Chiara came to visit us in America, we invited friends to a special dinner in her honor. Before we went to bed, I found her in the kitchen opening a can of tomatoes. She was homesick for pasta with tomato sauce.

Not that pasta is a fallback: *oh, let's just make a pasta.* Ordinary and daily as it is, pasta remains something to relish. The romance in this long marriage stays alive. What's the secret?

Possibly, memory. Each time the pasta pot steams brings memories of all the other times the windows fogged. When the son calls from the valley below and says, *"Butta la pasta,"* throw on the pasta, "I'm almost home," anticipation rises through the house. When you ladle the smoky *al fumo* sauce over the *pici,* you sense the presence of *nonna,* who taught you. When you stir the *ragù,* so innate that you never learned it at all, you can taste your whole life.

Most people eat pizza, also a birthright food, on Sunday night, after the momentous midday *pranzo* with the family. Although it can be a *primo,* usually pizza is really a solo event, something on its own and prepared very simply.

But still there's room for more in the soulful *primi* category. Tuscan home soups are little known to the traveler. Menus offer minestrone and *ribollita,* but rarely dip a ladle into the home cook's cauldron. Kale, White Bean, and Sausage Soup on a frosty day, Yellow and Red Pepper Soup when you're feeling holy, summery Pappa al Pomodoro, or Garlic Soup, to complement the roast—the range of intensely flavorful soups surprises many who know *primi* mostly through pastas.

Give Italians a song and they make arias, give them a car and they make a Maserati, give them rice and they transform it into risotto. This import from the north feels firmly at home in the Tuscan kitchen.

The first risotto I ever met was soon after college when an Italian colleague served it with asparagus. I still remember the creamy texture, the saffron tint, the crisp asparagus, and the deeper taste of the Parmigiano that she swirled in at the end. "Don't try to make it," she said. "You won't find the rice." She brought it back from vacations and saved it for parties, where she'd dazzle us with strange creations such as ossobuco and ravioli. Hard to imagine now, when our markets stock items from all over the world. Rice is a long-time comfort food. I used to eat plain buttered rice when I was lonely. As a Deep South child, I preferred rice and gravy over mashed potatoes and gravy—heresy. Rice always has been important in my pantheon of culinary deities, so experimenting with all kinds of risotto in Italy is a pleasure.

THE ART OF PASTA

Several friends who are accomplished bakers balked at making pasta, but once they saw the process, they couldn't believe how easy and quick it is. It takes about thirty minutes. Even in Tuscany, most people opt for *pastasciutta*, dried pasta, or buy their *cavatelli* or ravioli at the fresh pasta shop, getting out the rolling pin only for Sunday lunch. Most towns have *pasta fresca* shops; along with the *forno*, the bread shop, I consider these to be shrines to the household gods.

Making pasta by hand seems meditative; to pulse it a few turns in the food processor is *veloce*—fast. Either way produces fine results. I think the handmade is slightly superior in texture.

BASIC PASTA

2½	CUPS ALL-PURPOSE FLOUR, PLUS ADDITIONAL FOR KNEADING
3	EGGS
1	TEASPOON SALT
2	TEASPOONS EXTRA-VIRGIN OLIVE OIL
1 TO 2	TABLESPOONS WATER, PLUS ADDITIONAL IF NEEDED

BY HAND: Mound the flour on a countertop, and form a well in the middle. Beat the eggs in a small bowl, then pour them into the well with the salt, olive oil, and 1 tablespoon of water. Mix with a fork, gradually adding the flour as you go, until most of it is incorporated. Then knead the dough until it is smooth, about 10 minutes. Add more water if the dough feels too dry. Shape into a flattened disk. Cover it with a damp dishtowel and let it rest for at least 30 minutes.

BY FOOD PROCESSOR: In a small bowl, beat together the eggs, salt, olive oil, and 1 tablespoon of water. Place the flour in the bowl of a food processor fitted with a steel blade and add the egg mixture, pulsing until the mixture just starts to form a ball. Add more water if the dough feels too dry. Turn the dough out onto a floured surface and knead as described above. Shape into a flattened disk. Cover it with a damp dishtowel and let it rest for at least 30 minutes.

Divide the disk into four wedges—don't try to roll out the whole disk. Flour a work surface. How much flour? In Italian recipes, often you read *q.b.* or *q.s.*, *quanto basta* and *quantum sufficit*—whatever's enough. Just a light dusting for the work surface, the rolling pin, and your hands.

The fun starts here. Roll out the dough about ⅛ inch thick and then cut what you want—wide strips for lasagne or thin strips for tagliatelle. While you roll out the other three wedges, you can loop the pasta over the rungs of a folding clothes dryer or a broom handle propped between two chairs. Or sprinkle a little polenta on the pasta and lay it between sheets of plastic wrap on a cookie sheet. If new pasta is stacked on a tray, it will stick together.

We use a hand-cranked pasta machine and find it easier than wielding the rolling pin. Feed one of the four wedges of pasta into the machine on the lowest setting, then on the next highest setting. Keep running the strip through on consecutively higher settings, up to the second-to-last setting, or until almost transparent pieces unfurl and the pasta is about 36 inches long. You feel like you're pulling scarves out of a hat. One recipe of pasta makes four of these swaths—enough for a big lasagne, a generous pan of cannelloni, or about forty small ravioli.

One of our favorite shapes is *fazzoletti*, little handkerchiefs. Cut 5-inch squares, and cook them five or six at a time for 1 to 2 minutes. Top three or four on a plate with a few spoons of pesto, ragù, or vegetable sauce—sublime and very tender. Very little goes to waste in a Tuscan kitchen. Leftover bits of pasta are spontaneously shaped and called *maltagliata*, badly cut. They're cooked and enjoyed as much as the well-formed tortellini or *cavatelli*.

You can feed the swaths of pasta back through the machine's cutting devices to make tagliatelle, fettuccine, or whatever shapes your machine has. These will need to be hung to dry for an hour before they're cooked.

DRIED PASTA

Which to prefer—fresh or dried? Both—they're different. Every Italian grocery store bears witness to the taste for the immensely various shapes of *pasta asciutta*. What playful names: *mezze maniche* (short sleeves), *radiatori* (radiators), *strozzaprete* (priest stranglers), *stellete* (little stars), *orecchiette* (little ears), *penne* (pens), *vermicelli* (little worms), *linguine* (little tongues), *farfalle* (butterflies), *cavatappi* (corkscrews), and dozens more. Nothing is handier than a shelf lined with your favorites; a quick meal waits right there. What a surprise to find that a bowl of spaghetti with extra-virgin olive oil, grated cheese, and lots of pepper is a favorite in Rome. That seems as elemental as one of those ancient columns you encounter there. Maybe because Italians like pasta itself, they use much less sauce than most of us are used to in the United States.

COOKING PASTA

The guideline is 6 quarts of water for 1 pound of pasta. But, really, who's measuring? Fill a big pasta pot half full if you're cooking a half pound (serving two or three), and three-quarters full for a pound or more. Bring the water to a rolling boil. This takes around twenty minutes for a full pot, so time the cooking with your sauce preparation. Salt the water only when it boils. For 1 pound of pasta, throw in 2 tablespoons of salt. The water will

grab it and sizzle for a moment. Add the pasta and stir a few times to prevent sticking. Bring the water back to a boil if the pasta has tamed it. The salty water will season the pasta perfectly. Applying salt to the exterior later isn't as good.

Freshly made pasta cooks in a flash—1, 2, or 3 minutes depending on whether it's lasagne or ravioli. For dried pasta, time it as the package says, but take a taste before the suggested time elapses. Italians prefer pasta quite al dente, "to the tooth," or slightly resistant. If destined for *pasta al forno*, drain dried pasta just when it has lost that hard interior core; it will continue cooking in the oven. No matter what preparation you're using, I recommend frequent tasting.

I used to serve sauce over pasta. In Italy, I learned to quickly drain the pasta when it's ready, and then return it to the empty pot. Never rinse pasta. Toss in part of any cheese you're using, and then mix in most of the warm sauce, keeping a little to spoon on top when you serve the plates. This way, the cheese and sauce coat the still-starchy pasta.

Do as the Tuscans do and always reserve some pasta water, in case you want more liquid in your sauce. Just scoop out a cup before draining the pot. The starchy water helps the sauce cling to the pasta. Pasta water is especially useful for *pasta al forno*, such as the Baked Pasta with Sausage and Four Cheeses (page 91) or a macaroni and cheese, since when uncovered in the oven, these are exposed to dry heat.

SERVING SIZE: Portion size is subjective. Our recipes suggest that 1 pound of pasta serves six as a *primo* and four as a main course. Most boxes of pasta say "Serves 8," a small serving indeed.

Giusi's RAGÙ

S low and easy—long-simmered *ragù* is the quintessential Tuscan soul food. There are as many ways with *ragù* as there are cooks. This is ours, learned originally from Giusi, who's made it a thousand times. By now, I think we have, too. On many Saturday mornings, Ed makes a huge pot of *ragù*—tripling, quadrupling the recipe—and another of tomato sauce. We consider these our natural resources. For lunch, while the pots are still on the stove, we spoon *ragù* over *bruschetta*, add some cheese, and run it under the broiler. By afternoon, we're ready to fill several glass containers of different sizes and freeze them. We're then free to pull one out during the workweek.

Serve *ragù* in lasagne or over spaghetti and, as you eat, you know you're participating in a communal rite that's being enacted all over the Italian peninsula.

SERVES 10

       3 TABLESPOONS EXTRA-VIRGIN OLIVE OIL
       1 POUND GROUND LEAN BEEF
       1 POUND GROUND PORK
       2 ITALIAN SAUSAGES, CASINGS REMOVED
       1 TEASPOON SALT
      ½ TEASPOON PEPPER
       2 TEASPOONS FRESH THYME LEAVES OR 1 TEASPOON DRIED
  1 TO 2 CUPS RED WINE
       1 CUP *SOFFRITTO* (PAGE 20)
       2 TABLESPOONS TOMATO PASTE
16 TO 20 TOMATOES OR 2 28-OUNCE CANS WHOLE TOMATOES, JUICE
          INCLUDED, CHOPPED

Pour the olive oil into a 4-quart heavy pot with a lid. Over medium-high heat, brown the meats, breaking up the sausage with a wooden spoon, about 10 minutes. Add the salt, pepper, thyme, and 1 cup of the red wine. After the wine has cooked into the meat, about 10 minutes, add the *soffritto*, and stir in the tomato paste and tomatoes.

Bring the sauce to a boil, and then lower to a quiet simmer. Partially cover, and continue cooking for 3 hours, stirring now and then. Along the way, add the remaining cup of wine if you think the sauce is too dense.

TRENETTE *with* PESTO *and* POTATOES

SERVES 4 TO 6

3   SMALL POTATOES, PEELED AND DICED
2   TABLESPOONS SALT
½   POUND GREEN BEANS, TOPPED AND TAILED,
     CUT INTO THIRDS
1   POUND TRENETTE OR TROFIE PASTA
1   RECIPE PESTO (PAGE 26)
½   CUP (2 OUNCES) GRATED PARMIGIANO-REGGIANO
     SALT AND PEPPER TO TASTE

Along the Ligurian coast, pesto is hallowed. The rippled variety of basil that grows in that area has a particular kick. When we go to Portofino, we order the local specialty, trofie pasta cooked with potatoes and green beans, all tossed in fresh pesto. Sitting with them by that breathtaking harbor, drinking a slightly spritzy white wine, and feasting on this pasta—this qualifies as heaven.

If you were Ligurian, you'd cook the potatoes along with the pasta, which nicely coats the pasta with more starch. I'm afraid of overcooking the potatoes, so I steam them, then add them to the pot just before the pasta is done. I cook the green beans with the pasta because they're more predictable. Short tapered twists of trofie are the pasta of choice in Liguria. I prefer rippled strands of trenette, but both are perfect.

Bring the pasta water to a boil in a large pasta pot. In a small saucepan, boil the potatoes until barely done, about 3 minutes.

When the water starts to boil, add the salt, the green beans, and the pasta. When they're almost done, 8 to 10 minutes, add the nearly done potatoes to the pasta and stir them in. When the pasta is just al dente, drain it quickly, reserving some pasta water. Return the trenette mixture to the pot. Stir in the pesto and the Parmigiano. Taste to see if it needs any salt or pepper. Since the pesto is seasoned and the pasta water is salted, it probably will not. Add a little pasta water if you think it needs some. Serve quickly.

Ivan's PEAR AGNOLOTTI *with* GORGONZOLA *and* WALNUTS

SERVES 6

   BASIC PASTA (PAGE 68)
1 EGG YOLK BEATEN WITH 1 TABLESPOON WATER,
   FOR EGG WASH

FOR THE FILLING

2 TEASPOONS EXTRA-VIRGIN OLIVE OIL
1 LARGE NEARLY RIPE PEAR, SUCH AS A BOSC,
  PEELED, CORED, AND CUT IN LARGE DICE
⅓ TEASPOON SALT
⅓ TEASPOON PEPPER
1 CUP (8 OUNCES) WHOLE-MILK RICOTTA
¾ CUP (3 OUNCES) GRATED PARMIGIANO-REGGIANO
1 WHOLE EGG
  A FEW GRATINGS OF NUTMEG

FOR THE CREAM SAUCE

4 TABLESPOONS (½ STICK) UNSALTED BUTTER
7 OUNCES GORGONZOLA, IN CHUNKS
½ CUP HEAVY CREAM

10 WALNUT HALVES, TOASTED AND CHOPPED

Delicatissimo, this pasta. And so is the act of making it: the floury crimped moons, the pale filling, then the folded puffs, as soft as dandelions you blow to the wind and wish upon. It feels more like a poem than a pasta. But then the taste delivers a punch: the pungent cheese, ricotta with its hint of hay, and the airy perfume of pear.

Prepare the filling. In a small pan, heat the olive oil over medium-low and add the pear, salt, and pepper. Cook for 3 minutes, until the pears are barely fork tender, and set aside to cool. In a medium bowl, beat the ricotta, Parmigiano, egg, and nutmeg. Fold in the pears.

Roll out the pasta, and with a water glass or other round cutter, make circles 2½ to 3 inches in diameter.

Place about 2 teaspoons of the pear filling in the center of half of the pasta circles. Brush the egg wash around the edges. Cover each with another circle of pasta. Crimp all around with the tines of a fork in order for the two circles to adhere.

Prepare the cream sauce. Over low heat, melt the butter in a small saucepan. Add the Gorgonzola. When the cheese has melted, add the cream. Keep the cream sauce warm over low heat.

Boil the water, salt it, and drop in the circles. Return to a boil, then cook until the pasta floats to the top and the edges are tender, about 3 minutes. Spoon the pasta onto the plate, top with the sauce, and scatter the walnuts on top.

Silvia's PASTA *with* DUCK SAUCE

SERVES 8 TO 10

1	DUCK, 3 TO 4 POUNDS
¼	CUP EXTRA-VIRGIN OLIVE OIL
½	POUND GROUND BEEF
2	ITALIAN SAUSAGES, CASINGS REMOVED, SLICED
½	CUP *SOFFRITTO* (PAGE 20; ½ RECIPE)
1½	CUPS DRY WHITE WINE
1	TABLESPOON TOMATO PASTE
8 TO 10	TOMATOES OR 1 28-OUNCE CAN WHOLE TOMATOES, JUICE INCLUDED, CHOPPED
½	TEASPOON SALT
½	TEASPOON PEPPER
2	POUNDS TAGLIATELLE OR PAPPARDELLE
1	HANDFUL OF FLAT-LEAF PARSLEY, CHOPPED
½	CUP (2 OUNCES) GRATED PARMIGIANO-REGGIANO

At Riccardo and Silvia Baracchi's idyllic inn, Il Falconiere, outside Cortona, a falcon on a perch welcomes guests to their serene kingdom. Since they opened the inn around the same time as we bought Bramasole, we've grown up together. On their terrace with bowers of roses and a profile of Cortona in the distance, Ed and I, with fifty friends, celebrated our twentieth anniversary of owning Bramasole, with many toasts to the Baracchis as well.

Silvia and Riccardo respect Tuscan food traditions and their noble property, which was once owned by a poet and falconer. They have added their own refined and playful style. The romantic dining room centers on a tapestry of a woman with a falcon on her wrist, riding a horse. Metaphorically, Silvia is now the woman in the tapestry, leading the way through fantastic meals, with experimental flourishes based on local ingredients.

Wash and dry the duck, removing all innards.

Cut the duck into six pieces. Discard the skin and fat from the breasts. Remove fat from the other pieces, but leave on the skin.

Finely chop the breasts and set aside.

In a 12-inch skillet with a lid or an 8-quart heavy saucepan over medium heat, add the olive oil and remaining duck pieces, browning them on all sides, about 5 minutes. Add the duck breast, ground beef, sausages, and *soffritto*. Break up the beef and sausages with a wooden spoon, and brown all the meat, about 8 minutes.

Raising the heat to medium high, add the wine, and cook rapidly until the liquid is reduced just enough to cover the bottom of the pan, about 10 to 13 more minutes. Stir in the tomato paste and tomatoes to the pan, lower the heat to a simmer, and cook, covered, for 1 hour, turning the duck pieces a few times. Check occasionally to see if there's sufficient liquid in the pan; if not, add some of the reserved liquid from the canned tomatoes. If you use fresh tomatoes, add some water or another splash of white wine.

After 1 hour, season the sauce with salt and pepper. Simmer it an additional 25 to 30 minutes to thicken it. Remove the pan from the heat, and take out the duck pieces.

Bring the pasta water to a boil in a large pot.

When cool enough to handle, remove the duck meat from the bones and discard them. Chop the meat coarsely, and add it back to the pan. Cover and warm over medium-low heat.

Salt the pasta water, then cook and drain the pasta. Immediately add it to the simmering duck sauce, stirring to coat it well. Stir in the parsley. Warm the pan another 2 to 3 minutes, and pour the pasta into a big, warm bowl. Serve immediately. Pass the Parmigiano.

ORECCHIETTE *with* SHRIMP

SERVES 4 TO 6

- 1 CUP SHELLED PEAS
- 4 TABLESPOONS EXTRA-VIRGIN OLIVE OIL
- 3 SMALL FRESH SPRING ONIONS, FINELY CHOPPED
- 1 TEASPOON SALT, PLUS MORE FOR THE PASTA
- ¾ TEASPOON PEPPER
- ¾ POUND ORECCHIETTE
- 1 POUND MEDIUM SHRIMP OR SMALL PRAWNS, PEELED AND CLEANED
- 4 GARLIC CLOVES, PEELED AND SMASHED
- ½ CUP WHITE WINE

This combination is amusing because of the similar shapes of the pasta and the shrimp. An immersion blender is handy for small purées right in the bowl. You can use young *fave*, if available, instead of peas.

Bring the pasta water to a boil in a large pasta pot.

In a large skillet over medium-low heat, cook the peas in 1 tablespoon of olive oil, about 3 minutes, and then add the chopped onions to the pan. Cook until the onions are soft and the peas are barely tender, about 3 more minutes. Remove to a small bowl, season with half the salt and pepper, and purée.

When the pasta water begins to boil, add salt and the orecchiette. Orecchiette cook longer than most pastas, about 12 minutes.

In the same skillet, sauté the shrimp in the remaining olive oil with the garlic and the rest of the salt and pepper. When the shrimp turn pink, after 3 to 4 minutes, add the white wine, turn the heat to high for 1 minute, and then turn it off and discard the garlic.

When al dente, drain the pasta, reserving some water, and return it to the pot. Add the shrimp and peas, along with about ⅓ cup of the reserved pasta water. Toss well and serve.

PICI *with* FRESH FAVA BEANS

SERVES 4 TO 6

Pici is Cortona's favorite pasta. Mine, too. Silvia taught us to form the long strands, three or four times the thickness of spaghetti. At Trattoria Toscana, Chef Santino serves it *all'aglione,* with a lot of garlic and bread-crumbs. Debora and Arnaldo, at Pane e Vino, serve pici with anchovies and breadcrumbs. When pici is on the menu, Ed can go no farther. Silvia invented this recipe for her restaurant, and her addition of *fave* is typical of her touch. Tuscans have been saying *fave* since 1221. Those beans Jack planted were inevitably *fave*—the only bean Europe had before the great culinary heists from America began.

FOR THE EGGLESS PASTA DOUGH

2 CUPS ALL-PURPOSE FLOUR, PLUS ADDITIONAL FOR KNEADING

2/3 TO 3/4 CUP WATER, PLUS ADDITIONAL IF NEEDED

1 TABLESPOON EXTRA-VIRGIN OLIVE OIL
PINCH OF SALT

FOR THE SAUCE

7 TABLESPOONS EXTRA-VIRGIN OLIVE OIL

2 GARLIC CLOVES, CHOPPED

2 CUPS CHERRY TOMATOES, QUARTERED

1/2 TEASPOON SALT

1/2 TEASPOON PEPPER

1/2 CUP YOUNG FAVA BEANS, STEAMED UNTIL BARELY DONE

6 TO 8 BASIL LEAVES, TORN

1/2 TEASPOON MINCED FRESH ROSEMARY OR 1/4 TEASPOON DRIED

1/2 TEASPOON FRESH THYME LEAVES OR 1/4 TEASPOON DRIED

1/2 CUP FRESH BREADCRUMBS, CRISPED IN 1 TABLESPOON EXTRA-VIRGIN OLIVE OIL

1/2 CUP (2 OUNCES) GRATED PECORINO

Make the eggless pasta dough. Mound the flour on a board and make a well in the center. Into the well add the water, olive oil, and salt. Slowly mix these into the flour, adding more water, if needed, as the dough comes together. Knead about 10 minutes until the dough is smooth. You are aiming for a soft but not sticky mix, but don't worry if the dough is stiff; it will relax while it rests. Form the dough into a log, cover loosely with a dishtowel, and set aside for 20 minutes.

When ready, cut the dough crosswise into very thin pieces or just pull off little chunks. With your hands, roll each piece into a snake about the thickness of a chopstick and up to 2 feet long. Continue until all the dough has been rolled. If some break, that just contributes to the homemade look. Leave the pici uncovered on the kitchen counter while you prepare the sauce.

Make the sauce. Heat 6 tablespoons of the olive oil over medium heat in a 4-quart saucepan. Add the garlic, and cook for 1 minute, until it is soft but not browned. Add the cherry tomatoes, salt, and pepper. Cook on medium heat for a couple of minutes.

Stir in the *fave*, and then the herbs. Turn the heat to low, and let this blend for 2 more minutes. Transfer the mixture to a small bowl. (You can then prepare the breadcrumbs in the same pan.)

Meanwhile, bring a large pot of water to a rolling boil, salt it, and drop in the pici. Boil for about 5 minutes, depending on thickness. They will have risen to the top. Taste to see if they are al dente, and then, with a slotted skimmer, transfer them to the pan with the breadcrumbs, tossing to coat the pici. Add the tomatoes and *fave* mixture and the handful of pecorino. Toss well, briefly warm everything, and serve immediately.

Pane e Vino's PICI *with* BREADCRUMBS *and* ANCHOVIES

SERVES 4 TO 6

Arnaldo Rossi's Trattoria Pane e Vino, in Cortona, draws a wine-savvy crowd to its brick-arched interior. When he opened his doors ten years back, he brought with him an up-to-the-minute knowledge of the wine explosion developing in our area. He's continued to present simple food that nudges tradition and at the same time honors the artisan cheese and *salume* makers. We have enjoyed the many wine-and-food pairing dinners Arnaldo and Marco, of Enoteca Molesini, sponsor. The winemaker comes and shares his stories, and the dinner shows off each wine. The tables sparkle with dozens of glasses, and the strangers at your table become friends.

This is Ed's favorite pasta at Pane e Vino. With it, he likes a sauvignon blanc such as Villa Russiz, Collio DOC, or a Poliziano Rosso di Montepulciano.

6	TABLESPOONS EXTRA-VIRGIN OLIVE OIL
1	HOT RED PEPPER, MINCED, OR PEPERONCINI (RED PEPPER FLAKES) TO TASTE
10	ANCHOVY FILLETS, CHOPPED
2	GARLIC CLOVES, MINCED
¼	CUP WHITE WINE
1	POUND HANDMADE PICI (SEE PAGE 78)
½	CUP COARSE FRESH BREADCRUMBS, CRISPED IN A LITTLE EXTRA-VIRGIN OLIVE OIL

Bring the pasta water to a boil and add salt.

Heat the olive oil in a large skillet, and add the red pepper, anchovies, and garlic. "Melt" over low heat for 5 minutes. Stir in the wine, and continue to blend everything, until the wine cooks down slightly and the anchovies dissolve into it, about 5 minutes.

Meanwhile, cook the pasta. When the pasta is al dente, drain, and stir it into the pan with the other ingredients. Add the breadcrumbs and toss.

Ann Cornelisen's PASTA with ARUGULA and PANCETTA

SERVES 4 TO 6

1	POUND SPAGHETTI
1½	CUPS HEAVY CREAM
½	TEASPOON SALT
½	TEASPOON PEPPER
1	BUNCH OF ARUGULA, CHOPPED
½ TO ¾	CUP (2 TO 3 OUNCES) GRATED PARMIGIANO-REGGIANO
8	SLICES PANCETTA, COOKED AND CRUMBLED

Bring the pasta water to a boil, salt it, and then add the spaghetti. Cook until al dente and drain, reserving ½ cup of the pasta water.

While the pasta is cooking, in a large skillet over low heat, combine the cream with the salt and pepper. When the pasta is done, add the arugula to the cream, and let heat for 3 to 4 minutes. Stir in the drained pasta and Parmigiano. Add the pasta water, then, just before serving, incorporate the pancetta. Serve immediately.

The wonderful prose stylist Ann Cornelisen lived in Cortona for twenty-five years. She was our close friend in our first years in Italy, and I dedicated *Under the Tuscan Sun* to her. If you've never read *Torregreca* and *Women of the Shadows*, I highly recommend both. Ann didn't like to cook, but she had a few specialties. Her pasta with arugula is on my top five pastas list—for its taste first, but also because it is *molto veloce*, very fast.

With this, Ed likes to serve Frescobaldi Morellino di Scansano Chianti Rufina Nipozzano.

PASTA SHELLS *with* SHRIMP *and* THREE CHEESES

SERVES 4 TO 6

When I was honored with an award from Barilla—no, not for eating the most pasta—I invented this recipe for the ceremonial dinner, using Barilla's jumbo shells. We make it also with Pasta di Gragnano's lumaconi (big snail shells), known in Italy as *conchiglia*, conch.

When filled with shrimp, these shells may provoke a round of applause when you bring them to the table. For a main course, sauté some more shrimp and surround the pasta shells on each plate with four or five more.

1	POUND (ABOUT 24) MEDIUM SHRIMP, PEELED AND CLEANED
5	TABLESPOONS EXTRA-VIRGIN OLIVE OIL
¾	TEASPOON SALT
½	TEASPOON PEPPER
24	LARGE PASTA SHELLS
2	EGGS, LIGHTLY BEATEN
½	CUP (2 OUNCES) GRATED PARMIGIANO-REGGIANO
2	CUPS (1 POUND) WHOLE-MILK RICOTTA
1½	CUPS (6 OUNCES) SHREDDED MOZZARELLA
1	TABLESPOON ROASTED GARLIC OR 2 GARLIC CLOVES, MINCED
10 TO 12	BASIL LEAVES, TORN, PLUS SEVERAL MORE WHOLE LEAVES FOR GARNISH
	JUICE OF 1 LEMON
1	CUP FRESH BREADCRUMBS, TOASTED
3	TOMATOES, CHOPPED

Preheat the oven to 350°F. Bring the pasta water to a boil and add salt.

In a large skillet over medium heat, sauté the shrimp in 1 tablespoon of the olive oil until barely pink, about 3 minutes. Season with half the salt and pepper.

Cook the pasta according to the package directions, taking care not to overcook. Cook a few extra shells in case of breakage. Drain and with a large metal spoon, carefully toss the shells with 1 tablespoon of the olive oil in a large bowl. Set aside.

In a small bowl, combine the eggs with the 3 cheeses, garlic, half of the remaining salt and pepper, and half of the basil. With a teaspoon, gently stuff each shell with some of the cheese mixture. Press 1 shrimp onto each. Arrange in a 9 x 13-inch oiled baking dish. Mix the lemon juice with 2 tablespoons of the olive oil and dribble it over the shells. Sprinkle the breadcrumbs on top. Bake for 15 minutes.

Prepare the tomatoes. In a small saucepan over medium heat, cook them briefly, 3 to 5 minutes, in the remaining 1 tablespoon olive oil. Stir in the remaining basil and the rest of the salt and pepper.

Serve the shells on a bed of tomatoes and garnish with the whole basil leaves.

SMOKY PASTA

SERVES 4 TO 6

- ¼ CUP EXTRA-VIRGIN OLIVE OIL
- ½ POUND *PANCETTA AFFUMICATA* (SMOKED), GROUND OR FINELY CHOPPED
- 1 GARLIC CLOVE, MINCED
- 1 TEASPOON MINCED FRESH ROSEMARY OR ½ TEASPOON DRIED
- 1 YELLOW ONION, FINELY CHOPPED
- ¼ CUP WHITE WINE
- 4 TABLESPOONS TOMATO PASTE
- 1½ CUPS TOMATO SAUCE (PAGE 21; ½ RECIPE)
- 1 POUND PENNE
- ⅓ CUP HEAVY CREAM
- ½ CUP (2 OUNCES) GRATED PARMIGIANO-REGGIANO

Bring the pasta water to a boil.

Heat the olive oil in a large skillet over medium heat, and add the pancetta. Cook for 5 minutes, or until crisp. Remove the pancetta and drain on a paper towel. Add the garlic, rosemary, and onion to the pan, cooking until the onion slightly colors, about 3 minutes.

Add the white wine to the pan. Cook for 2 to 3 minutes, and then stir in the tomato paste and the tomato sauce. Lower the heat and simmer, covered, for another 10 minutes.

In the meantime, salt the water and cook the penne until al dente.

Stir the cream into the sauce. It should be concentrated, but if it seems too dense, add up to ½ cup of pasta water. Heat through and toss with the pancetta, penne, and Parmigiano.

If *pancetta affumicata*, Italian smoked bacon, is not available, use regular bacon. That stash of tomato sauce made on Saturday quickly sends this Monday night *pasta affumicata* to the table. Use penne rigate, the striated penne, instead of the smooth, because the sauce adheres to it. If the smoked pancetta is ground, it bonds well to the pasta.

The Grattamacco Bolghieri Rosso holds its ground with *pasta affumicata*.

ANGRY PASTA

All'arrabbiata ramps up the taste of classic pasta with tomato sauce and basil. Use fresh tomatoes, if possible.

With this hot pasta, pair a smooth syrah such as Amerighi Cortona Syrah.

1	YELLOW ONION, FINELY CHOPPED
2	TABLESPOONS EXTRA-VIRGIN OLIVE OIL
2	GARLIC CLOVES, FINELY CHOPPED
8	TOMATOES OR 1 28-OUNCE CAN WHOLE TOMATOES, CHOPPED
1	TEASPOON SALT
½	TEASPOON PEPPER
½	TEASPOON PEPERONCINI (RED PEPPER FLAKES), PLUS ADDITIONAL TO TASTE
½	CUP PITTED BLACK OLIVES, HALVED
1	POUND PENNE RIGATE (STRIATED), SPAGHETTI, PICI, OR BUCATINI
¾	CUP (3 OUNCES) GRATED PARMIGIANO-REGGIANO
1	HANDFUL OF FLAT-LEAF PARSLEY, CHOPPED
6 TO 8	BASIL LEAVES, TORN

Bring the pasta water to a boil and add salt.

In a large skillet, over medium-low heat, cook the onion 4 to 5 minutes in the olive oil, adding the garlic for the last minute. Add the tomatoes, salt, pepper, red pepper flakes, and olives to the pan. Bring to a boil and then reduce the heat to a solid simmer. Cook for 15 minutes, stirring occasionally, until the sauce is slightly reduced. Taste the sauce to see if you want more red pepper heat.

Meanwhile, cook the pasta and drain. Stir the Parmigiano into the pasta, then add the tomato sauce, along with the parsley and basil. Toss well and serve.

SPAGHETTI *with* LEMON *and* CRAB

SERVES 4 TO 6

1	POUND SPAGHETTI
1	POUND CRABMEAT
2	TABLESPOONS EXTRA-VIRGIN OLIVE OIL
¼	CUP WHITE WINE
½	CUP LEMON JUICE
½	TEASPOON SALT
¼	TEASPOON PEPPER
½	CUP (2 OUNCES) GRATED PARMIGIANO-REGGIANO
½	CUP FLAT-LEAF PARSLEY, CHOPPED

To this pasta, I usually add a pound of crab, but it's also marvelous without. With a green salad, it's the lightest dinner imaginable—perfect for the day after a crippling feast.

In Tuscany, I think you have to go to confession if you scatter grated cheese over pasta with seafood. It's not done. *Mea culpa*, I like the Parmigiano with lemon and crab.

Bring the pasta water to a boil, salt it, and add the pasta.

While the pasta cooks, add the crabmeat to the olive oil in a large skillet over low heat, and just warm it briefly. Add the wine, bring it quickly to a boil, and immediately turn the heat to low. Stir in the lemon juice and seasonings.

Drain the pasta, reserving ½ cup of pasta water. Pour the pasta into the pan with the crab. Toss in ¼ cup of the Parmigiano and the parsley. If the pasta needs more liquid, add a little of the reserved pasta water. Serve in bowls, sprinkling the remaining Parmigiano on top.

THE FRAGRANCE OF SUNLIGHT

If I had to name the one ingredient I must have in the kitchen, it would be the lemon. The flavor, both assertive and enhancing, is like liquid sunshine blending into the food. As an essential of the Italian garden, lemons are so valued that most old houses have a *limonaia*, a glass-walled room where the pots bask in sunlight and are protected from winter cold. Even in February, I can squeeze between the branches and find an emergency lemon. In spring, we drag the trees out in front of the house again, to a place near the kitchen door—very handy for picking a juicy lemon for this extremely easy and tasty pasta.

When the pots are wheeled out again, they're all positioned exactly as they were. Fabio marks each pot so the orientation to the sun will be the same. I wondered why, with so many lemons grown this way, they were not a common ingredient in the Tuscan repertoire. Beautiful they are, but did no Tuscan ever shout "Eureka!—crab and lemon," or even "lemonade"? Later I learned how smart the Italians were long before vitamin deficiencies were discovered. They raised citrus for medicinal purposes.

POTATO RAVIOLI *with* ZUCCHINI, SPECK, *and* PECORINO

MAKES ABOUT 40 SMALL RAVIOLI; SERVES 6 AS A *PRIMO*

At Corys, the hotel-restaurant down the road from Bramasole, this sunny ravioli is always on the menu. Here, Chef Eva Seferi shares her secret recipe.

Speck (smoked prosciutto) can be used in all the ways prosciutto is used. Substitute Parmigiano-Reggiano if you can't locate aged pecorino. For Eva's ravioli, you can purchase fresh sheets of pasta or you can make your own.

FOR THE FILLING

½ POUND YUKON GOLD POTATOES, PEELED AND CUBED
1 CUP WHOLE MILK
1 CUP WATER
1 TABLESPOON GRATED PARMIGIANO-REGGIANO
1 EGG YOLK
½ TEASPOON SALT
A FEW GRATINGS OF NUTMEG

BASIC PASTA (PAGE 68)
1 EGG YOLK, LIGHTLY BEATEN, FOR EGG WASH

FOR THE SAUCE

3 TABLESPOONS EXTRA-VIRGIN OLIVE OIL
2 SLICES SPECK OR SMOKED BACON, DICED
1 ZUCCHINI, CHOPPED
2 TOMATOES, CHOPPED
1 SHALLOT, MINCED
1 TABLESPOON UNSALTED BUTTER
½ TEASPOON PEPPER

PECORINO, SHAVED, AS NEEDED

Make the filling. In a small saucepan over medium-low heat, cook the potatoes in the milk and water for 20 minutes. When just fork-tender, drain them, reserving some of the cooking liquid. Pass the potatoes through a ricer into a medium bowl, and add the Parmigiano, egg yolk, salt, nutmeg, and enough of the cooking liquid, approximately 3 tablespoons, to make a lightly firm filling. Mix well and let cool.

After the pasta dough has rested for 30 minutes to an hour, divide it into quarters, and follow the process described on page 68.

Bring the pasta water to a boil and add salt.

Place 1 pasta sheet on a lightly floured countertop. On the lower half of the sheet, place 1 teaspoon of the potato filling at 2½-inch intervals. Brush the egg wash on the top half of the sheet, and then fold it over, covering the filling. Gently press out any air in the ravioli, and then cut them into equal squares with a knife, a rolling pizza cutter, or a pastry crimper. Pinch the edges together to seal. Continue this method with the remaining pasta sheets.

Cook the ravioli in the boiling water for 2 to 3 minutes after they float to the surface, and then lift them from the water with a slotted spoon. Reserve ½ cup of the water for the sauce.

Make the sauce. In a large skillet over medium-low heat, heat the olive oil, and then add the speck. Cook for 1 minute, then add the zucchini, tomatoes, and shallot. Continue cooking for 5 minutes, turning the vegetables several times. Add the butter, pepper, and reserved ½ cup of pasta water and cook for 5 minutes.

Carefully add the ravioli to the pan. Spoon some sauce over them and heat through, about 3 minutes. Serve on plates, scattering shavings of pecorino over the ravioli.

LASAGNE *with* RAGÙ

SERVES 8

Buy or make fresh pasta, if possible. If not, look for an artisan dried pasta.

Hearty Siro Pacenti Rosso di Montalcino complements this equally hearty lasagne.

3 CUPS *RAGÙ* (PAGE 70)
2 CUPS *BESCIAMELLA* (PAGE 24; RECIPE DOUBLED)
BASIC PASTA (PAGE 68) OR 1 POUND DRIED LASAGNE
½ CUP (2 OUNCES) GRATED PARMIGIANO-REGGIANO
2 CUPS (8 OUNCES) SHREDDED MOZZARELLA
½ CUP COARSE FRESH BREADCRUMBS, TOASTED
2 TABLESPOONS EXTRA-VIRGIN OLIVE OIL, FOR THE BAKING DISH AND TOP LAYER OF PASTA

Preheat the oven to 350°F.

Prepare the *ragù* and the *besciamella*.

Bring the pasta water to a boil, salt it, and cook the pasta two sheets at a time for 1 to 2 minutes, if fresh. (If you're using dried pasta, follow the recommended cooking time but subtract a minute.) Fill a large bowl with cold water. Carefully lift out the lasagna sheets with a large slotted spoon and stop the cooking by dipping the pasta in the water. If any tear, they can be used for middle layers. Spread each sheet on a dishtowel.

To assemble, oil a 9 x 13-inch baking dish (one you'll serve from), and layer the ingredients by first spooning a little *ragù* on the bottom, followed by a layer of pasta, then *besciamella* (about ⅓ cup) then Parmigiano, then mozzarella. Pace the amounts for five layers of pasta, *ragù* (about ½ cup), *besciamella*, Parmigiano, and mozzarella. End with a layer of pasta. Dab the top with *ragù*, sprinkle on the breadcrumbs, and dot with olive oil. Bake, uncovered, for 30 minutes, or until the lasagne is bubbling around the edges and the top looks toasty.

I could write a book on lasagne, or at least a few sonnets. An old favorite, pesto lasagne, has about a hundred calories a bite. Worth every morsel! The cooked pasta is layered with pesto, *besciamella*, and Parmigiano, and topped with breadcrumbs. Another beauty comes from the Abruzzo—layer the pasta with *besciamella*, Parmigiano, and lots of tiny veal meatballs (see page 128).

Some other winning combinations for vegetable lasagne are:

Zucchini and Tomatoes

Eggplant, Peppers, and Caramelized Onions

Yellow, Red, and Green Peppers in Separate Layers

WILD MUSHROOM LASAGNE

SERVES 8

    BASIC PASTA (PAGE 68) OR ¾ TO 1 POUND DRIED
    LASAGNE
2   CUPS *BESCIAMELLA* (PAGE 24; RECIPE DOUBLED)
2   GARLIC CLOVES, MINCED
1   TEASPOON FRESH THYME LEAVES OR ½ TEASPOON DRIED

FOR THE FILLING
6   TABLESPOONS EXTRA-VIRGIN OLIVE OIL
1   SMALL ONION, FINELY CHOPPED
4   CUPS WILD MUSHROOMS, SLICED (PREFERABLY PORCINI)
1   TEASPOON SALT
½   TEASPOON PEPPER
⅓   CUP WHITE WINE
1½ CUPS (6 OUNCES) GRATED PARMIGIANO-REGGIANO
½   CUP FRESH BREADCRUMBS, CRISPED IN EXTRA-VIRGIN
    OLIVE OIL

Preheat the oven to 350°F.

Oil a 9 x 13-inch baking dish and cut the pasta to fit. The middle layers can be irregular. Bring the water to a boil and add salt.

Simmer the *besciamella* with the garlic and thyme just to let the flavors meld.

To a large skillet over medium-high heat, add 4 tablespoons of the olive oil and the onion. Sauté for 1 minute and then add the mushrooms. Stir them for 3 minutes. Add the salt, pepper, and wine. Raise the heat just briefly to a boil, and then remove the pan from the stove.

Drop the pasta sheets one by one into the boiling water and cook until barely done, 1 to 2 minutes for fresh pasta. With tongs, gently remove the pasta, dip in cold water, and let them briefly dry on dishtowels. Reserve ½ cup of the pasta water.

Place a layer of pasta in the baking dish. Cover the bottom layer with a thin layer of *besciamella,* a scattering of mushrooms, and a sprinkling of cheese. Repeat the process, reserving ¼ cup of Parmigiano. Add a little pasta water to the *besciamella* if you've used too much on the first layers. Top the dish with the breadcrumbs and Parmigiano. Drizzle over it the remaining 2 tablespoons olive oil. Bake, uncovered, for 30 minutes, until the edges are bubbling and the breadcrumbs are browned.

When you taste mushroom lasagne, you remember the scent of the forest floor after a warm rain.

Thin sheets of fresh pasta create a light, light lasagne. After I watched a real pro with pasta in a local shop, I began to roll my pasta much thinner. Hers was like a bedsheet and very supple.

Wild mushrooms are so flavorful that 4 cups will be enough—just dot them over the *besciamella.* If you don't have wild mushrooms, use more—6 cups of cultivated mushrooms perked up with 1 ounce of dried porcini that have been soaked for 30 minutes in stock, tepid water, wine, or cognac, then squeezed, drained, and chopped.

For wine, if you like rosé, I suggest the flowery but dry Mazzei, IGT Toscano Belguardo Rosé. A good choice for a red wine is Poggio di Sotto's Rosso di Montalcino.

BAKED PASTA *with* SAUSAGE *and* FOUR CHEESES

SERVES 4 TO 6

- 1 TABLESPOON EXTRA-VIRGIN OLIVE OIL, PLUS ADDITIONAL FOR THE BAKING DISH
- ½ POUND SWEET ITALIAN SAUSAGE, CASINGS REMOVED, MEAT CUT INTO SMALL PIECES
- ½ POUND SPICY ITALIAN SAUSAGE, CASINGS REMOVED, MEAT CUT INTO SMALL PIECES
- ½ CUP RED WINE
- 2 TEASPOONS FRESH OREGANO LEAVES OR 1 TEASPOON DRIED
- 1 CUP *SOFFRITTO* (PAGE 20)
- ½ TEASPOON SALT
- ½ TEASPOON PEPPER
- 8 TOMATOES OR 1 28-OUNCE CAN WHOLE TOMATOES, JUICE INCLUDED, CHOPPED
- 1 POUND RIGATONI
- 1 CUP (8 OUNCES) WHOLE-MILK RICOTTA
- 8 OUNCES FONTINA OR TALEGGIO, CUBED
- 8 OUNCES MOZZARELLA, CUBED
- ½ CUP (2 OUNCES) GRATED PARMIGIANO-REGGIANO
- ½ CUP FRESH BREADCRUMBS, TOASTED

With the bread oven hot, we slide many different dishes across the brick floor—focaccia, pork loins, and of course, baked pastas. Ed adapted this recipe for kitchen use. We've served this at a hundred casual suppers. I don't think there's a better pasta.

For this most robust pasta, our local wine seller, Marco Molesini, recommends a Super Tuscan, such as Guidalberto from Bolgheri, made by Tenuta San Guido of Sassicaia fame.

Preheat the oven to 375°F.

Bring the pasta water to a boil and add salt.

In a large skillet, heat 1 tablespoon of the olive oil over medium heat and cook the sausage, breaking it up as it browns, about 5 minutes. Add the red wine, turn the heat up to boil, and cook until much of the liquid has reduced, about 10 minutes. Add the oregano, *soffritto,* seasonings, and tomatoes along with their juices. Simmer the sauce for at least 10 minutes, or until thick and savory.

Cook the rigatoni a minute less than the time required on the package (since it will continue cooking in the oven), then drain, reserving a bit of the pasta water.

In a large bowl, mix the ricotta with the fontina and a splash of the pasta water, then add the drained rigatoni and continue mixing. Add the sausage mixture and mozzarella, tossing to mix well.

Oil a 9 x 13-inch baking dish, and then pour in the pasta. Sprinkle the Parmigiano and breadcrumbs on top. Bake uncovered for 25 minutes or until golden flecked and hot.

GARLIC SOUP

SERVES 4

No cause for alarm—the copious amount of garlic in this recipe is attenuated by the simmering, during which the strength dissipates but the flavor stays. Serve this soup warm or chilled, topped with toasted croutons or a slice of *bruschetta*.

2 MEDIUM POTATOES, PEELED AND DICED
1 YELLOW ONION, CHOPPED
2 TABLESPOONS EXTRA-VIRGIN OLIVE OIL
2 WHOLE HEADS OF GARLIC, PEELED
5 CUPS CHICKEN STOCK
½ TEASPOON SALT
½ TEASPOON PEPPER
1 TABLESPOON FRESH THYME LEAVES OR
  1½ TEASPOONS DRIED
½ CUP HEAVY CREAM
  SNIPPED CHIVES, FOR GARNISH

Steam the potatoes, about 10 minutes. In a 6-quart heavy saucepan over medium heat, sauté the onion in the olive oil. When it begins to turn translucent, in a few minutes, add the garlic and turn the heat to low. The garlic should soften but not brown—cook gently, about 15 minutes.

Add the potatoes to the onion and garlic, along with 1 cup of the chicken stock. Season with the salt and pepper. Bring just to a boil, then quickly lower the heat and simmer very gently for 20 minutes. Purée with an immersion blender and add the remaining 4 cups of stock and the thyme. Stir with a whisk and simmer for 20 minutes to blend flavors. Whisk in the heavy cream. Serve warm or chilled. Stir before serving. Scatter the snipped chives on top.

YELLOW *and* RED PEPPER SOUP

SERVES 8

- 2 RED BELL PEPPERS
- 2 YELLOW BELL PEPPERS
- 1 YELLOW ONION, MINCED
- 2 TABLESPOONS EXTRA-VIRGIN OLIVE OIL
- ½ TEASPOON SALT
- ½ TEASPOON PEPPER
- 1 LARGE POTATO, PEELED AND CUBED
- 4 CUPS CHICKEN STOCK
- 1 CUP CROUTONS
- 1 TEASPOON FRESH THYME LEAVES OR ½ TEASPOON DRIED
- 1 CUP (8 OUNCES) MASCARPONE

Usually there's not much drama in a soup bowl, but here the separate yellow and red pepper soups are ladled simultaneously into a bowl so that one half is yellow; the other, red. Topped with a few herbed croutons, this is as intriguing to the eye as it is to the palate. When I don't have access to a grill, I char the peppers over the stove's flame, turning frequently with long tongs.

Grill the peppers until charred, either over a grill or the stove's flame. Put them in a paper bag to cool and sweat. In a small pan over medium heat, cook the onion in 1 tablespoon of the olive oil, the salt, and pepper until the onion is translucent, 2 or 3 minutes. Reserve the onions and leave the pan for toasting the breadcrumbs. In another small saucepan, boil the potato in 1 cup of water, partially covered, until fork tender. Drain the potatoes and reserve the water.

Peel all the char away from the peppers. You don't want black spots in the soups. Cut the peppers into quarters and clean out the seeds and ribs.

Pour 1 cup of the stock into a food processor. Add half of the onion, half of the potato, half of its starchy water, and the quartered yellow peppers. Purée until smooth. Pour this into a medium saucepan. Repeat with the red peppers, the other half of the onion and potato, and the water, pouring the purée into a separate saucepan.

Into each soup stir in another cup of stock. Simmer for 20 minutes on medium-low heat, stirring now and then. Adjust the seasonings if necessary.

In the pan the onion was cooked in, heat the other tablespoon of olive oil and brown the croutons over low heat for 3 to 4 minutes, adding the thyme.

Before serving, whisk ½ cup of mascarpone into each soup and continue to heat. With two ladles (or two cups) and a little fortitude, dip into each soup and empty the ladles simultaneously and steadily, so that the soups meet in the bowl but don't mix. Float three or four croutons on each and glide to the table.

PAPPA *al* POMODORO

SERVES 4

A treat of high summer, when the teepees of tomato plants are laden, *pappa al pomodoro*, bread with tomatoes, is the simplest of all simple soups—and definitely more than the sum of its parts. In a restaurant, I have ordered a second bowl and skipped the rest of the meal.

- 2 YELLOW ONIONS, FINELY CHOPPED
- 1 CELERY STALK AND ITS LEAVES, MINCED
- 1 CARROT, MINCED
- 3 TABLESPOONS EXTRA-VIRGIN OLIVE OIL
- 8 SLICES DAY-OLD RUSTIC BREAD
- 3 CUPS VEGETABLE STOCK
- 8 TO 10 TOMATOES, SEEDED AND CHOPPED
- 15 TO 20 BASIL LEAVES, TORN
- SALT AND PEPPER TO TASTE

Sauté the onions, celery, and carrot in the olive oil in a 6-quart saucepan over medium heat. When just done, place the bread on top. Add a cup of stock and bring to a boil, breaking the bread apart with forks. Simmer, and as the bread absorbs the liquid, add the remaining 2 cups of stock, the tomatoes, basil, salt, and pepper, and simmer for 15 minutes, or until the deep red soup is thick and velvety.

MINESTRONE: BIG SOUP

3   YELLOW ONIONS, CHOPPED
3   CARROTS, CHOPPED
3   CELERY STALKS WITH LEAVES, CHOPPED
¼   CUP EXTRA-VIRGIN OLIVE OIL
1   BUNCH OF RED OR GREEN CHARD, INCLUDING STEMS,
    CHOPPED VERY WELL
1   HANDFUL OF FLAT-LEAF PARSLEY, CHOPPED
1   TABLESPOON FRESH THYME LEAVES OR
    1½ TEASPOONS DRIED
1   CUP WHITE OR RED WINE
8   CUPS CHICKEN STOCK
8   TOMATOES OR 1 28-OUNCE CAN WHOLE TOMATOES,
    CHOPPED
3   TABLESPOONS TOMATO PASTE
1   CUP OVEN-ROASTED TOMATOES (SEE PAGE 42) OR AN
    ADDITIONAL 1 CUP OF CHOPPED FRESH TOMATOES
    HEEL OF A WEDGE OF PARMIGIANO-REGGIANO
3   POTATOES, PEELED, CUBED, AND STEAMED
    SALT AND PEPPER TO TASTE
1   CUP (4 OUNCES) GRATED PARMIGIANO-REGGIANO

In a large stockpot over medium heat, sauté the onions, carrots, and celery in the olive oil for 5 to 7 minutes, or until almost done. Add the chard, parsley, and thyme and mix. Pour in the wine and stock, and stir in the chopped tomatoes, tomato paste, and oven-roasted tomatoes. Bring to a near boil. Throw in the heel of Parmigiano, cover the pot, and then reduce the heat to low so the soup barely bubbles for 45 minutes. Give it an occasional stir. Add the potatoes and remove from the heat. Season to taste.

Pass the grated Parmigiano at the table.

Winter's favorite song. Even better the next day. The *-one* suffix means "big." The secret of soup is balance—not too much of any one ingredient. Instead of potatoes, you could substitute a pasta, such as small macaroni, but I would not use both.

If I say *"zuppa"* to Nunziatina at the *frutta e verdura*, she piles everything I'll need into my bag, plus handfuls of fresh parsley and basil. I take her advice to include the heel of the Parmigiano. Once cooked, the softened heel is the cook's treat.

A pot of minestrone on the stove: you're home.

RIBOLLITA

A thick, soul-stirring soup with white beans, leftover bread, and vegetables. As the translation, "reboiled," indicates, this is a soup that is easily made using leftovers, probably from a Sunday dinner. The classic recipe calls for hunks of bread to be added to the pot at the end. Tuscans drip extra-virgin olive oil into each bowl at the table. Leftover pasta, green beans, peas, pancetta, and potatoes can all be added to the pot the next day.

The soup, with a salad, is a complete meal—unless you've been out plowing.

1	POUND DRIED CANNELLINI BEANS, RINSED (SEE PAGE 24)
2	TEASPOONS SALT
2	YELLOW ONIONS, DICED
6	CARROTS, DICED
2	TABLESPOONS EXTRA-VIRGIN OLIVE OIL, PLUS ADDITIONAL FOR THE TABLE
4	CELERY STALKS, DICED
4 TO 5	GARLIC CLOVES, MINCED
1	TEASPOON PEPPER
1	BUNCH OF KALE OR CHARD, FINELY CHOPPED
8 TO 10	TOMATOES OR 1 28-OUNCE CAN WHOLE TOMATOES, CHOPPED
	HEEL OF A WEDGE OF PARMIGIANO-REGGIANO
2	QUARTS VEGETABLE, CHICKEN, OR MEAT STOCK
2	CUPS (OR MORE) CUBED DAY-OLD BREAD
	GENEROUS HANDFUL OF COMBINED CHOPPED FLAT-LEAF PARSLEY, TORN BASIL, AND THYME LEAVES
1	CUP (4 OUNCES) GRATED PARMIGIANO-REGGIANO

Prepare the cannellini beans (see page 24). Let them cook until almost done. They will continue cooking in the next step. Stir in 1 teaspoon of the salt.

In a stockpot over medium-low heat, sauté the onions and carrots in the olive oil. After 3 or 4 minutes, add the celery, garlic, remaining 1 teaspoon salt, the pepper, and kale. Add more olive oil if needed. Cook for 10 minutes or until the kale is wilted, and then add the tomatoes, the heel of the Parmigiano, and the drained beans. Add enough stock to cover. Bring to a boil, and then simmer, covered, for 1 hour to blend the flavors. Stir now and then. Add the bread cubes and herbs. Heat through and serve with the grated Parmigiano and olive oil to pass around the table.

ONION SOUP
in the AREZZO STYLE

SERVES 8

- 6 LARGE YELLOW ONIONS, THINLY SLICED
- 4 TABLESPOONS (½ STICK) UNSALTED BUTTER
- 1 QUART VEGETABLE STOCK
- 1 TEASPOON SALT
- ½ TEASPOON PEPPER
- 20 SLICES TUSCAN-STYLE BREAD
- 8 SLICES FONTINA (ABOUT 6 OUNCES)
- 1 CUP (4 OUNCES) GRATED PARMIGIANO-REGGIANO

Soup you can eat with a fork! On a rainy day in Arezzo, we ordered this at the café wine bar, La Torre di Gnicche, where owner Lucia Fioroni told us it is the soup locals have been enjoying for hundreds of years. She quickly wrote down the recipe. We made it the next day, and now it's a cold-weather necessity.

Preheat the oven to 350°F.

In a large saucepan over medium-low heat, cook the sliced onions in the butter until they're beginning to soften, about 10 minutes. Add the stock, salt, and pepper. Bring to a boil, then lower the heat to a simmer. Cover and cook for about 10 minutes, until the onions are cooked through.

Butter two 9 x 5-inch loaf pans or an 8 x 12-inch baking dish with a 3-inch depth. Line the ends and bottoms of the pans with bread slices and spoon in a layer of onions and stock. Add 4 fontina slices to each pan, then another layer of bread and stock. Sprinkle generously with Parmigiano. Bake in the oven for 30 minutes. Serve hot in a shallow bowl. It's even better the next day.

KALE, WHITE BEAN, *and* SAUSAGE SOUP

SERVES 12

Kale goes by another name, black cabbage—*cavolo nero*—which sounds much more dashing, like a black cavalier. It's also called dinosaur kale (*lacinato*), maybe because its knobby leaves look like the back of a lizard.

Do not confuse *cavolo*, accent on first syllable, with *cavallo*, accent on second, or you'll be ordering black horse. This substantial soup is a balm for the spirit.

2 ITALIAN SAUSAGES, CASINGS REMOVED
1/4 CUP EXTRA-VIRGIN OLIVE OIL
2 YELLOW ONIONS, CHOPPED
2 GARLIC CLOVES, MINCED
2 QUARTS CHICKEN STOCK
1 CUP WHITE WINE
1 TEASPOON FRESH THYME LEAVES OR 1/2 TEASPOON DRIED
1 BUNCH KALE, STALKS INCLUDED, WASHED AND CHOPPED
1/2 TEASPOON SALT, PLUS ADDITIONAL TO TASTE
1/2 TEASPOON PEPPER
4 CUPS COOKED CANNELLINI BEANS (PAGE 24)

In a stockpot over medium heat, brown the sausages in 2 tablespoons of the olive oil, breaking them up with a wooden spoon. Remove to a bowl. Add the remaining 2 tablespoons of oil along with the onions and garlic, and cook on medium-low heat until translucent. Add the chicken stock and wine, and raise the heat to medium for 15 minutes. Stir in the thyme, kale, salt, and pepper. Bring to a boil. Cover and lower the heat to simmer for 15 minutes. Add the sausage and beans, and simmer another 10 minutes. Taste, in case you need more salt.

TWO TASTY RISOTTOS

Like pasta, risotto is endless in variety. A special local risotto is made with nettles. Evil as they are when mature, they're a spring treat when very young. Simply chop and quickly blanch them, then stir them into the risotto at the last minute of cooking.

I especially like risotto with *fave* that have been briefly sautéed with minced shallots, and then stirred into the risotto. Other good choices are:

CHOPPED FENNEL, BARELY COOKED,
WITH SAUTÉED SHRIMP

———

SAUTÉED FRESH MUSHROOMS,
OR DRIED PORCINI SOAKED IN TEPID
WATER UNTIL PLUMPED

———

TALEGGIO, GRILLED RED RADICCHIO,
AND PANCETTA

———

CHARD, RAISINS, AND PINE NUTS

———

SHAVINGS OF TRUFFLE AND A LIGHT
DUSTING OF GRATED
PARMIGIANO-REGGIANO

———

A DOUBLE RECIPE OF *SOFFRITTO*
AND CUBES OF FONTINA

———

ROASTED BUTTERNUT SQUASH
AND ONION

In Italy, you can buy porcini bouillon cubes in grocery stores. They're excellent for risotto when no stock is at hand. If you travel there, tuck a few boxes in your luggage on the way back.

Many recipes call for too much butter; if you have a good stock, butter is unnecessary and only a little excellent olive oil is needed to start things off.

SHRIMP RISOTTO

SERVES 8

A dd cooked crab claws, steamed clams, and mussels to this recipe for a bountiful seafood risotto.

1   YELLOW ONION, MINCED
3   TABLESPOONS EXTRA-VIRGIN OLIVE OIL
1   TEASPOON SALT
½   TEASPOON PEPPER
2   CUPS (1 POUND) CARNAROLI OR ARBORIO RICE
8   CUPS (CHICKEN OR VEGETABLE) STOCK
1   CUP WHITE WINE
1   POUND WILD-CAUGHT MEDIUM SHRIMP, PEELED AND CLEANED
1   HANDFUL OF FLAT-LEAF PARSLEY, CHOPPED
1   TABLESPOON SNIPPED CHIVES

In a heavy 6-quart pan over medium heat, sauté the onion in 1 tablespoon of the olive oil for 3 minutes, adding the salt and pepper. Add the rice and cook, stirring, for 3 to 4 minutes to coat the grains. Meanwhile, in another large pot, bring the stock and wine to a boil, and then lower the heat to a simmer. Ladle the stock gradually into the rice, stirring each ladleful of liquid into the rice until it is absorbed before adding more. Keep both the remaining stock and the rice at a simmer.

In a medium skillet, sauté the shrimp in the remaining 2 tablespoons olive oil until done, about 4 minutes.

Stir and stir until the rice is done, about 20 minutes. This risotto is best when left rather soupy. Combine the shrimp, rice, parsley, and chives. Serve immediately.

RISOTTO PRIMAVERA

SERVES 6

3	POUNDS FRESH PEAS, SHELLED
1	BUNCH OF SLENDER CARROTS, PEELED
2	BUNCHES OF ASPARAGUS
5½	CUPS CHICKEN STOCK
½	CUP WHITE WINE
2	CUPS (1 POUND) CARNAROLI OR ARBORIO RICE
1	YELLOW ONION, FINELY CHOPPED
1	TABLESPOON EXTRA-VIRGIN OLIVE OIL
1	TEASPOON SALT, PLUS ADDITIONAL TO TASTE
1	TEASPOON PEPPER, PLUS ADDITIONAL TO TASTE
	JUICE AND ZEST OF 1 LEMON
½	CUP (2 OUNCES) GRATED PARMIGIANO-REGGIANO

"The best meal I've ever had," a friend said, after a simple dinner of risotto with spring vegetables. Of course, it wasn't, but the effect of a lovely mound of risotto in the middle of the plate surrounded by a wreath of colorful and flavorful vegetables inspires effusive declarations. This seems like the heart of spring dining. It must be what Botticelli's gossamer girls in *La Primavera* ate after prancing about the forest.

An ideal dinner: Risotto Primavera followed by roast chicken, served with lettuces tossed with pear slices and Gorgonzola. I suggest La Foa, a sauvignon blanc by Colterenzio, or Ronca di Mele by Venica & Venica, two of my favorites, as accompaniments.

Season all of the vegetables with salt and pepper. Briefly steam the peas. If not slender, cut the carrots into pieces about the same size as the asparagus stems. Cook the carrots until barely done. Break the asparagus stalks just where they naturally snap and steam or roast them. The vegetables should remain crisp.

In a large saucepan, heat the stock and wine to a boil, and then turn down to a simmer. In another heavy 6-quart pot, sauté the rice and onion in the olive oil for a couple of minutes over medium heat, stirring to coat and brown the rice. Add 1 teaspoon each of the salt and pepper and gradually ladle in the stock as the rice absorbs the liquid. Keep stirring and ladling in more liquid until the rice is done, about 20 minutes. Some prefer their risotto almost soupy, but for this dish it is better moist and almost al dente.

Remove from the heat, add the zest and lemon juice, stir in the Parmigiano, and season to taste. Serve the rice immediately in large shallow bowls with the vegetables surrounding the rice.

RISOTTO SALTATO

SERVES 4

Leftover risotto is a bonus and, crisped in a skillet, rivals the original presentation. Risotto Saltato makes a great breakfast. The title sounds salty, but *saltato* actually means "sautéed," or, etymologically, from *saltare*, "to jump."

In a hurry? Just sauté leftover risotto in hot olive oil and sprinkle with Parmigiano.

2   TABLESPOONS EXTRA-VIRGIN OLIVE OIL
4   CUPS LEFTOVER RISOTTO
1   CUP (4 OUNCES) SHREDDED MOZZARELLA
½   CUP TOMATO SAUCE (PAGE 21)

In a 10-inch nonstick pan with a lid, set over medium-low heat, heat the olive oil. When the oil is hot, add 2 cups of the risotto, spreading it flat with a spatula. Add half the mozzarella, and pour over it the tomato sauce. Top with the rest of the mozzarella, and finish with the other 2 cups of risotto. Sauté for 10 minutes. The risotto will crisp on the bottom. Invert onto the pan lid, and slide the uncooked side back into the pan. If the rice sticks to the pan, use a wide spatula and turn it in 2 or 3 sections, then just pat it back together. Cook for another 5 minutes.

If the risotto sticks to the bottom of the pan, just cover the pan, lower the heat, and cook for 5 minutes more. It will still be crisp on the bottom. Serve immediately.

PIZZA

Pizza inspires creativity. Ed's favorite is Napoli: capers, anchovies, mozzarella. I like fontina, olives, and prosciutto. Another favorite is arugula and curls of Parmigiano. If you use arugula as a topping, don't add it until the pizza is cooked. We're also enamored of potato pizza, as well as all the standard ones. A great vegetarian combination is grilled eggplant with sun-dried tomatoes, olives, oregano, basil, and mozzarella.

For variety, you can make your own version of *quattro stagioni*, four seasons, pizza. The classic is artichokes (spring), green peppers (summer), mushrooms (fall), and prosciutto (winter). Other good choices are oven-roasted tomatoes with sausage or black olives and pancetta. We suggest keeping the toppings simple. Italian pizza never has big mixtures of ingredients—only one or two, such as capers and anchovies.

If you see *pizza capricciosa* on the menu, you're at the caprice of the chef, who may break an egg into the center of the pizza as it comes out of the oven. The heat barely cooks the egg.

For a party, we cut three kinds of pizza into wedges. It's a super antipasto that complements most casual dinners, or serves as a simple dinner by itself—pizza crosses all courses.

Ivan's PIZZA MARGHERITA

MAKES TWO 14-INCH ROUND PIZZAS

The first pizza out of our bread oven is the classic Margherita, the plainest of pizzas, but the most loved in our area, possibly because of veneration for a local miracle worker, Santa Margherita, whose preserved body still lies behind glass in the church named for her.

The dough should be thin so it will crisp but remain flaky and tender.

FOR THE PIZZA DOUGH

- 1 PACKAGE ACTIVE DRY YEAST (1/4 OUNCE)
- 1 CUP WARM WATER, 110° TO 115°F
- 3 1/2 CUPS ALL-PURPOSE FLOUR, PLUS ADDITIONAL FOR KNEADING
- 2 TABLESPOONS EXTRA-VIRGIN OLIVE OIL
- 2 TEASPOONS SALT

FOR THE TOMATO SAUCE AND TOPPING

- 2 TABLESPOONS EXTRA-VIRGIN OLIVE OIL
- 8 FRESH TOMATOES OR 1 28-OUNCE CAN WHOLE TOMATOES, DRAINED AND CHOPPED
- 1 TABLESPOON FRESH OREGANO LEAVES OR 1 1/2 TEASPOONS DRIED
- 1/2 TEASPOON SALT
- 1/2 TEASPOON PEPPER

- 2 CUPS (8 OUNCES) SHREDDED MOZZARELLA
- 10 FRESH BASIL LEAVES, TORN

Make the crust. Pour the yeast into the cup of water and let it sit for 10 minutes. Put the flour in a large bowl, and make a well. Add the olive oil and the salt. Mix in the water and yeast. Blend with a fork, pulling in the flour from the sides. The dough will begin to look like little rags. Continue mixing another 3 or 4 minutes, until a mass forms. Pile the dough on a floured counter and knead for 5 to 10 minutes, until the dough is smooth, then put it in a floured bowl. Slice a cross on the top (to help the dough rise), cover with a dishtowel, and let it swell until nearly doubled, about 1 hour.

Make the tomato sauce. In a medium bowl, combine the olive oil, tomatoes, oregano, salt, and pepper. Reserve a couple of pinches of oregano.

Divide the dough into two equal pieces. In a 14-inch pizza pan, spread out one piece of dough with your hands. Repeat with the other piece or freeze for later use. Let the pizza rest for 15 to 20 minutes.

Preheat the oven to 500°F.

Over each pizza, spread 1 cup of the tomato sauce, and bake for about 10 minutes. (You'll have a cup of tomato sauce left over.) Remove the pizza from the oven, and add half the mozzarella and the rest of the oregano. Return the pizzas to the oven for another 8 minutes or until the cheese is melted and the crust browned. Just as it comes out of the oven, scatter on the basil. For maximum success, Ivan insists that adding the cheese after a partial baking will produce a better texture. His method produces a flaky crust with browned edges.

PIZZA *with* CARAMELIZED ONION *and* SAUSAGE

MAKES TWO 14-INCH ROUND PIZZAS

PIZZA DOUGH (OPPOSITE)
EXTRA-VIRGIN OLIVE OIL, FOR BRUSHING THE DOUGH
4   YELLOW ONIONS, THINLY SLICED
2   TABLESPOONS EXTRA-VIRGIN OLIVE OIL
3   TABLESPOONS BALSAMIC VINEGAR
1   TEASPOON MARJORAM LEAVES OR ½ TEASPOON DRIED
    SALT AND PEPPER TO TASTE
2   CUPS (8 OUNCES) SHREDDED MOZZARELLA
3   ITALIAN SAUSAGES, CASINGS REMOVED

We use pork sausage seasoned with fennel seeds. This pizza is universally beloved in Tuscany.

Divide the dough into two equal pieces. With your hands, spread out each piece in a 14-inch pizza pan. Cover it with a dishtowel, and let it rest for 15 to 20 minutes.

In a medium skillet, covered, on low heat, "melt" the onions in the olive oil and balsamic vinegar for 20 minutes, stirring them frequently. The onions should be caramel-colored and limp. Season with the marjoram, salt, and pepper, and set aside.

Preheat the oven to 500°F.

Scatter the onions and cheese over the dough. Break the sausage into ½ teaspoon–size pieces and stud the pizza with them. Bake for 15 minutes or until the cheese is bubbling and the sausage is cooked.

SECONDI

Winter food here recalls the hunter stepping in the door with his jacket pockets filled with birds, the farmer bringing in the olive harvest. Fog fills the valleys. Tuscan food of this season calls for massive appetites. For us, long walks build us up to the hefty dishes that we order in *trattorie*: pasta with wild boar *ragù*, *lepre*, hare, fried mushrooms, and polenta. The rich smells drifting from our kitchen are different in winter. The light summer fragrances of basil, lemon balm, and tomatoes are replaced by aromas of succulent pork roast glazed with honey, guinea hens roasting under a layer of pancetta, and *ribollita*, that heartiest of soups. Subtle and earthy, the fine shavings of Umbrian truffle over a bowl of pasta prick the senses. At breakfast, the perfumed melons of summer are forgotten and we use leftover bread for slabs of French toast spread with plum jam I made last summer from the delicate *coscia di monaca*, nun's thigh, variety that grows along the back of the house. The eggs always startle me; they're so *yellow*. The freshness does make a tremendous difference, so that a platter of eggs soft-scrambled with pecorino and a big dollop of mascarpone becomes a very special treat.

I didn't anticipate the extent of the excitement of cooking in winter: the entire shopping list changes for the cold season. What's available, primarily, is what grows, though citrus does come up from the South and Sicily. A mound of tiny orange clementines, bright as ornaments, shines in a blue bowl on the windowsill. Ed eats two or three at a time, tossing the peels into the fire, where they blacken and shrivel, sending out the pungent scent of their burning oil. Because the days are so short, the evening dinners are long, and long prepared for.

—FROM *Under the Tuscan Sun*

SECONDI

CHICKEN UNDER A BRICK *116*

CHICKEN WITH OLIVES AND TOMATOES *117*

CHICKEN WITH ARTICHOKES, SUN-DRIED TOMATOES, AND CHICKPEAS *118*

QUAIL BRAISED WITH JUNIPER BERRIES AND PANCETTA *120*

PATRIZIA'S RABBIT *121*

RABBIT WITH TOMATOES AND BALSAMIC VINEGAR *123*

HONEY-GLAZED PORK TENDERLOIN WITH FENNEL *124*

ED'S PORK ROAST *125*

ROASTED VEAL SHANK *126*

ROLLED VEAL SCALLOPS FILLED WITH ARTICHOKES *127*

LITTLE VEAL MEATBALLS WITH ARTICHOKES AND CHERRY TOMATOES *128*

SHORT RIBS, TUSCAN STYLE *129*

OSSOBUCO *130*

PLACIDO'S STEAK *131*

"FINGER-BURNER" LAMB CHOPS *133*

ROAST LEG OF LAMB WITH HERBS AND PANCETTA *134*

BEEF TENDERLOIN WITH BALSAMIC VINEGAR *135*

RICH POLENTA PARMIGIANA WITH FUNGHI PORCINI *137*

POLENTA WITH SAUSAGE AND FONTINA *138*

PASTA FRITTATA *139*

GIUSI'S EGGPLANT PARMIGIANA *139*

FRITTO MISTO *140*

SEA BASS IN A SALT CRUST *142*

FISHERMAN'S FISH FOR LUNCH *143*

ROLLED SOLE WITH FENNEL AND CITRUS *144*

BRODETTO *145*

FRANCA'S SEA BASS *147*

PRAWNS AND CHERRY TOMATOES WITH PURÉE OF CANNELLINI *148*

FRANCES'S SUMMER SHRIMP SALAD *149*

Although I've read many times that Tuscans are known as "bean eaters," I'd say from my observations that Tuscans are more ardent meat eaters. Everyone I know cooks outside on a stone or brick grill, or on wrought-iron grills in the fireplace, where one of those slow-turning iron-spit contraptions whirrs, the skewer loaded. The old ones are spring wound, newer versions are electric. Pigeons, pork belly, guinea hen, liver, sausages, and hunks of lamb thread the skewer, a mix that is roasted over coals and then stripped off and onto a platter. The big *bistecca,* though, will be seared on a grill over a hotter flame.

"Fire!" Ed shouts as he comes up from the shed with a bundle of *scopa,* the dried brush from a type of heather called *l'erica* that is used to start the flames. "We need to see fire!" Soon everyone gathers around him and he spears *scottaditi,* the tiny lamb chops known as "finger-burners," onto the grill. I easily acquiesce to his handling this manly art, and turn to other courses. At Piero and Ombretta's annual Ferragosto party (August 15), Placido—seemingly effortlessly—grills about forty steaks. In winter, Ed and I like to cook a couple of veal chops in the fireplace at Bramasole, right where in times long past all the family's food was cooked. We still have a dented and blackened copper polenta cauldron, though we've never used it. We hauled to the United States one of the wrought-iron grills sold at every Tuscan market so that we could make good use of coals in the fireplace on late autumn evenings. In Tuscany, cooking with fire is so prevalent that it amounts to a way of life.

Chickens usually are shoved into the bread oven after the pizza frenzy finishes and the temperature mellows. Gilda cooks three or four at a time, along with a couple of tarts. Several friends still have wood-fired stoves in their kitchens, along with a gas stove. At appliance stores, I'm cheered to see such an array of these bright blue and red stoves and to know that they are still incredibly popular. They're used for a long-simmering *ragù* and ribs and for quick scaloppini. All winter the purring woodstove keeps the kitchen toasty. Instinctively, Domenica knows the temperature, as a mother does just by touching her child's forehead.

The ease of live roasting and grilling carries over into other *secondi.* Tuscan meats and fish are simple. Veal scaloppini is done in four minutes. Sear and flip, squeeze of lemon, a few capers, and that's that. Our own improvisations, such as veal chops stuffed with

pistachios and rosemary, follow that lead. We learned—continue to learn—to rely on dynamic combinations of a few flavors, rather than elaborate preparations. Reduced balsamic vinegar and bay leaf enliven a beef tenderloin, sage and a cube of fontina tuck into a meatball, fennel and citrus roll inside a sole fillet, juniper berries and shallots shift quail into a higher realm, and almonds, raisins, and saffron transform a sea bass. Tuscans are minimalists: less often *is* more. "What's in this?" we regularly ask a friend at dinner. Inevitably the recipe has only a few ingredients. "You don't want a muddle," Gilda explains.

As ever, the quality of the meat, fish, or fowl makes all the difference. Is the butcher one of your best friends?

CHICKEN *under a* BRICK

SERVES 4

1	CHICKEN, 3½ TO 4 POUNDS
2	GARLIC CLOVES, MINCED
1	HANDFUL OF FLAT-LEAF PARSLEY, CHOPPED
	ZEST FROM 1 ORANGE
¼	CUP EXTRA-VIRGIN OLIVE OIL
½	TEASPOON SALT
½	TEASPOON PEPPER
¼	CUP WHITE WINE

FOR THE MARINADE

2	TABLESPOONS RED WINE VINEGAR
½	CUP EXTRA-VIRGIN OLIVE OIL
½	CUP WHITE WINE
	SALT AND PEPPER TO TASTE

Weighing down a splayed chicken with bricks seems so ancient. Did a Roman Emperor hatch the slogan "A Chicken Under Every Brick" to go along with the Bread and Circuses motif?

Brick morphed so naturally from the good earth. Add water and high heat—*ecco fatto*, it's done—terracotta. And civilization starts to build in a big way. Any brick will do here. If you have a few handy, wash them, let them air-dry, and wrap them in aluminum foil. Or use a heavy pan of some sort, covering the bottom with foil.

Almost as easy as roast chicken, this has Tuscan flair and deep roots in the cuisine's history. Our Tuscan friends don't marinate the chicken, but the chicken is more succulent after its overnight immersion. Domenica's Rosemary Potatoes (page 171) go perfectly with this, as does Moris Farms Avvoltore from the Maremma.

Preheat the oven to 400°F.

Wash the chicken under cold running water and dry it. With poultry shears, remove the wingtips and any excess fat, and cut out the backbone. Put those aside for stock.

Combine the garlic and parsley in a small bowl with the zest, 2 tablespoons of the olive oil, ½ teaspoon salt, and ½ teaspoon pepper. Set aside.

In a large bowl, mix the marinade ingredients. Lay the chicken flat, skin side up, on your work surface. Stuff the garlic mixture under the skin and place the chicken in the marinade. Cover and refrigerate for a few hours or, even better, overnight. Turn it two or three times.

Heat the remaining 2 tablespoons of olive oil in a heatproof cast-iron pan large enough to hold the chicken. I use a 14-inch cast-iron skillet. Place the chicken breast side up and weight it down with two clean bricks wrapped in foil. Cook over medium heat for 10 minutes, and then place the pan and bricks in the oven for 20 minutes. Remove the weights and turn the chicken over, cooking another 20 minutes or so, until crispy and richly browned, about 50 minutes total. Remove the chicken to a platter and cut into serving pieces. Deglaze the pan with the wine and pour the juices over the chicken.

CHICKEN *with* OLIVES *and* TOMATOES

SERVES 4

- 5 TABLESPOONS EXTRA-VIRGIN OLIVE OIL
- 1 CHICKEN, 3 TO 4 POUNDS, CUT INTO 8 PIECES, DREDGED IN ABOUT ½ CUP FLOUR
- 1 TEASPOON SALT
- ½ TEASPOON PEPPER
- ½ CUP RED WINE
- 1 CUP MIXED BLACK AND GREEN OLIVES, PITTED
- 1 HANDFUL OF FLAT-LEAF PARSLEY, CHOPPED
- 1 CUP CHOPPED OVEN-ROASTED TOMATOES (SEE PAGE 42)

This is the little black dress in a cook's repertoire—always right.

Take Querciabella, Chianti Classico DOCG, a biodynamic wine, off the shelf for this olive-studded chicken.

Preheat the oven to 350°F.

Heat the olive oil in a large skillet over medium heat and brown the chicken pieces, 2 minutes on each side. Season with the salt and pepper. Add the wine, raise the heat to high for 1 minute, and then transfer everything to a 9 x 13-inch baking dish.

In a small bowl, mix the olives, parsley, and tomatoes, and pour this over the chicken. Bake uncovered for 30 to 45 minutes, depending on the size of the pieces, turning the chicken once.

CHICKEN *with* ARTICHOKES, SUN-DRIED TOMATOES, *and* CHICKPEAS

Stick a Post-it note on this recipe, and when in doubt, turn to it. The Mediterranean flavors transform "just chicken" into a memorable dinner.

Chickpeas are a late love of ours. Just a taste of chickpea fritters, which are a favorite Sicilian street food, and we were fans. Now we roast them for snacks, serve them with herbs and tomatoes as a cold salad, and adore them in this super-fast *piatto unico*, one-pot dinner.

Refer to the pantry section (page 17) for information on chickpeas. You can simmer them in light stock with onion, celery, carrot, and garlic, or just cook them in water and season afterward. Cooking chickpeas yourself yields a much better texture than you'll find in the soft and viscous canned ones. Artichokes partner well with the *ceci*. Although fresh artichokes are a primary passion, in this recipe I opt for the convenience of canned or frozen ones. If you're using sun-dried tomatoes in dry form, plump them for a half hour in wine or olive oil.

This hearty stew calls for a big wine, such as Tenuta Sette Ponti, IGT, Crognolo. All the Sette Ponti wines are terrific.

SERVES 6

- 5 TABLESPOONS EXTRA-VIRGIN OLIVE OIL
- 1 YELLOW ONION, CHOPPED
- 3 CHICKEN BREASTS, HALVED, SKIN ON
- 1 TEASPOON SALT
- ½ TEASPOON PEPPER
- ½ CUP RED WINE
- ¼ CUP CHOPPED FLAT-LEAF PARSLEY
- 2 CUPS COOKED CHICKPEAS (SEE PAGE 24)
- 2 14-OUNCE CANS WATER-PACKED ARTICHOKE HEARTS, DRAINED
- ½ CUP SUN-DRIED TOMATOES, SLIVERED, OR 1 CUP SLICED OVEN-ROASTED TOMATOES (SEE PAGE 42)
- ¼ CUP FRESH THYME OR FRESH MARJORAM LEAVES OR 2 TABLESPOONS DRIED
- ½ CUP BLACK OR GREEN OLIVES, PITTED

Preheat the oven to 350°F.

Over medium-low heat, in a large, enameled ovenproof pot with a lid, heat 1 tablespoon of the olive oil. Sauté the onion, and after about 3 minutes, remove it to a medium bowl. Season the chicken breasts with the salt and pepper. Add the remaining 4 tablespoons olive oil to the pot, raise the heat to medium-high, and brown the chicken for

3 minutes per side. Add the wine, bring it quickly to a boil, and then turn the heat off immediately.

Combine the onion with the parsley, chickpeas, artichoke hearts, sun-dried tomatoes, thyme, and olives. Spread the combined vegetables over the chicken, and bake, covered, for 30 to 40 minutes, depending on the size of the pieces, turning the chicken once. Serve right from the pot or transfer to a platter.

QUAIL BRAISED *with* JUNIPER BERRIES *and* PANCETTA

SERVES 6

12 QUAIL, PREPARED FOR COOKING
½ CUP ALL-PURPOSE FLOUR, FOR DREDGING
¼ CUP EXTRA-VIRGIN OLIVE OIL
1 TEASPOON SALT
½ TEASPOON PEPPER
¼ CUP BALSAMIC VINEGAR, OR MORE IF NEEDED
2 SHALLOTS, MINCED
12 STRIPS OF PANCETTA
8 SPRIGS OF THYME
1 TABLESPOON BLACK PEPPERCORNS, CRUSHED
1 TABLESPOON JUNIPER BERRIES, LEFT WHOLE
RED WINE, IF NEEDED

My father was a bird hunter, and our cook, Willie Bell, often was lost in a cloud of tiny feathers as she plucked a mound of quail. The drooping little heads all fell in the same direction. I wouldn't eat them, even after she smothered them with cream and pepper. With more equanimity, I've met them in Tuscany in a new guise.

The quail are excellent served with polenta, a parallel to Southern baked grits.

We first tried Arnaldo Caprai's Sagrantino di Montefalco over twenty years ago and have been loving it ever since.

Preheat the oven to 250°F.

In a paper bag, dredge the quail in the flour. In a large, heavy ovenproof pan with a tight-fitting lid, quickly brown the quail in the olive oil over medium heat for about 5 minutes. Season with the salt and pepper. Pour in the balsamic vinegar. Cover the quail with the shallots, then the strips of pancetta. Sprinkle with the thyme, peppercorns, and juniper berries. Roast, covered, for 2 hours, turning the quail over after about 1½ hours. Moisten now and then with a little red wine or more balsamic vinegar if they look dry. After 2 hours, check for tenderness. Continue to roast for another half hour if the quail are plump. They should be succulent and almost falling apart.

Patrizia's RABBIT

SERVES 6

1	3½-POUND RABBIT, BONED
8	OUNCES GROUND TURKEY
8	OUNCES GROUND PORK
8	OUNCES GROUND CHICKEN
1	EGG
½	CUP (2 OUNCES) GRATED PARMIGIANO-REGGIANO
1	HANDFUL OF BREADCRUMBS
2	GARLIC CLOVES, MINCED
	A FEW SPRIGS OF ROSEMARY AND SAGE, MINCED
1	SMALL BLACK OR WHITE TRUFFLE, MINCED, OR WHITE TRUFFLE PASTE (OPTIONAL, BUT GOOD)
1	TEASPOON SALT
1	TEASPOON PEPPER
	ENOUGH WHOLE MILK TO MOISTEN THE STUFFING, ½ CUP AT MOST
3	TABLESPOONS EXTRA-VIRGIN OLIVE OIL
¼	CUP WHITE WINE, PLUS MORE IF NEEDED

Preheat the oven to 350°F.

Wash and dry the rabbit. Lay it flat on a work surface. With a wooden spoon, combine well the turkey, pork, chicken, and egg in a large bowl. Work in the Parmigiano, breadcrumbs, garlic, herbs, truffle, and most of the salt and pepper. Moisten the stuffing with just enough milk to hold together.

Spread the stuffing on the rabbit, fold in the sides, and sew it with cooking thread or tie it with kitchen twine. Salt and pepper the outside. Wrap in a cheesecloth, tying each end with string. Place the stuffed rabbit in an oven pan, douse it with the olive oil and wine, and cook for 1½ hours. During the cooking, rotate the rabbit two or three times, basting it with the sauce that forms; if necessary, add more wine.

Allow the rabbit to come to room temperature. Cut away the cheesecloth. Slice the rabbit, arrange overlapping slices on a platter, and drizzle with the cooking juices.

We used to order *un bel coniglio ripieno*, a nice stuffed rabbit, for Sunday *pranzo* from Patrizia's *rosticceria*, which no longer exists. We still miss her, but fortunately, she gave us the recipe for her boneless stuffed rabbit. If your boning skills are rusty (or, like mine, nonexistent), you'll probably need to order a boned rabbit. This dish is especially attractive for a buffet supper; you can slice the whole thing so guests can easily serve themselves.

RABBIT *with* TOMATOES *and* BALSAMIC VINEGAR

SERVES 4

1	RABBIT, 2½ TO 3 POUNDS, CUT INTO SERVING PIECES
½	CUP ALL-PURPOSE FLOUR
¼	CUP EXTRA-VIRGIN OLIVE OIL
1	LARGE YELLOW ONION, CHOPPED
3 TO 4	GARLIC CLOVES, MINCED
8 TO 10	TOMATOES OR 1 28-OUNCE CAN OF WHOLE TOMATOES, CHOPPED
½	TEASPOON TURMERIC
½	TEASPOON MINCED FRESH ROSEMARY OR ¼ TEASPOON DRIED
½	TEASPOON SALT
½	TEASPOON PEPPER
½	TEASPOON FENNEL SEEDS, TOASTED
5	TABLESPOONS BALSAMIC VINEGAR
2	TABLESPOONS RED WINE VINEGAR

Preheat the oven to 350°F.

In a paper bag, dredge the rabbit in the flour. In a large skillet over medium-high heat, brown the pieces in 3 tablespoons of the olive oil, 2 to 3 minutes per side. Arrange them in a 9 x 13-inch baking dish.

Add the remaining 1 tablespoon of olive oil to the skillet, and on medium-low heat, cook the onion and garlic 1 to 2 minutes. Add the tomatoes, turmeric, rosemary, salt, pepper, and fennel seeds. Stir in both vinegars and simmer for 5 minutes. Pour the sauce over the rabbit.

Roast the rabbit, uncovered, for about 35 minutes. Midway through the cooking, turn over the pieces once. Check for doneness by cutting into a piece, as you would chicken.

*C*oniglio (rabbit) and *lepre* (hare) are staples of the Tuscan repertoire. Cooks in the country raise their own; hunters are pleased to bring home the wild *lepre*. At the Saturday market, we used to see a farm woman with three or four fluffy bunnies looking up from an old Alitalia flight bag. Now, in the butcher's case, they're more remote, clean and lean, ruddy pink, and it's no longer necessary to leave a bit of fur on the tail to prove it's not cat. Unappetizing as this note is, the rabbit, simmered in thick tomato sauce with herbs, is intensely savory. The recipe also works with chicken.

We like all of the Montecucco wines. For the richly flavorful rabbit, we recommend the Perazzeta, Licurgo Montecucco Rosso Riserva.

HONEY-GLAZED PORK TENDERLOIN *with* FENNEL

SERVES 4

The tenderest, leanest pork is the tenderloin. One serves two hungry people and loves partnerships with many ingredients. In short, second to chicken breast, it's the most versatile meat. Fennel, which especially pairs well with pork, grows all over our land. Whether its local popularity first came from its aphrodisiacal powers or its curative uses for eye problems, I don't know. I like its feathery foliage and its mythic connections. Prometheus is said to have brought the first fire to humans inside the thick, hollow stalk.

1 TABLESPOON FENNEL SEEDS
1 TABLESPOON MINCED FRESH ROSEMARY
   OR 1½ TEASPOONS DRIED
½ TEASPOON SALT
½ TEASPOON PEPPER
2 GARLIC CLOVES, MINCED
2 TABLESPOONS HONEY (LAVENDER OR ACACIA,
   IF AVAILABLE)
2 PORK TENDERLOINS, 1 POUND EACH
2 FENNEL BULBS, FRONDS RESERVED
¼ CUP WHITE WINE
½ CUP (2 OUNCES) GRATED PARMIGIANO-REGGIANO
   OR PECORINO
½ CUP (4 OUNCES) MASCARPONE
½ CUP FRESH COARSE BREADCRUMBS, CRISPED
   IN EXTRA-VIRGIN OLIVE OIL
   ROSEMARY WANDS, FOR GARNISH

Preheat the oven to 425°F.

In a mortar or food processor, crush the fennel seeds. In a small bowl, combine them with the rosemary, salt, pepper, and garlic. Reserve a teaspoon of this mixture for the fennel bulbs. Combine the rest with the honey, and spread this on the pork. Place in a shallow 8 x 12-inch parchment-lined pan. Roast in the oven until the pork is faintly pink in the middle, 20 minutes per pound, or to 145°F internal temperature, or to your desired state of doneness. Set the pork aside and cover to keep warm.

Lower the oven temperature to 350°F.

While the meat roasts, cut the fennel bulbs in ½-inch slices. Toss out the tough root end and reserve the fronds for garnish. Steam the fennel for about 10 minutes, until cooked but not soft. Transfer it to an oiled 7 x 10-inch baking dish.

In a small bowl, mix the reserved fennel-rosemary mixture with the wine, Parmigiano, and mascarpone. Spread this over the fennel and top with the breadcrumbs. Bake at 350° for about 10 minutes, until slightly browned and bubbling.

Slice the pork and arrange it on a large platter and spoon the fennel around it. Garnish the tenderloins with fennel leaves and with wands of fresh rosemary.

Ed's PORK ROAST

SERVES 6

- 1   BONELESS PORK LOIN, ABOUT 3 POUNDS
- 1   YELLOW ONION, MINCED
- 1   CUP FRESH BREADCRUMBS, CRISPED IN 2 TABLESPOONS
      EXTRA-VIRGIN OLIVE OIL
- ½   CUP (2 OUNCES) GRATED PARMIGIANO-REGGIANO
- 7   TABLESPOONS EXTRA-VIRGIN OLIVE OIL
- ¼   CUP RED WINE
- ½   CUP TORN BASIL LEAVES
- ½   CUP FLAT-LEAF PARSLEY, MINCED
- 2   TABLESPOONS FRESH THYME OR 1 TABLESPOON DRIED
- 3   TABLESPOONS MINCED FRESH ROSEMARY OR
      1½ TEASPOONS DRIED
- 3   TABLESPOONS FENNEL SEEDS
- 3   GARLIC CLOVES, MINCED
      ZEST OF 1 LEMON
- 1   TEASPOON SALT
- ½   TEASPOON PEPPER

If you're brining the pork, use a sharp knife to make a pocket in the pork loin before immersing it (see page 25). If you are skipping the brining, cut the pocket just before stuffing.

Preheat the oven to 350°F.

When you're almost ready to cook the pork loin, combine in a medium bowl the onion, breadcrumbs, Parmigiano, 5 tablespoons of the olive oil, the red wine, basil, parsley, thyme, rosemary, fennel seeds, garlic, lemon zest, salt, and pepper. Stuff half of the mixture in the pocket you've sliced, and tie the loin with kitchen twine in four or five places. Over medium-high heat, in a heavy 8-quart Dutch oven, heat the remaining 2 tablespoons olive oil and sauté the pork 4 min-

utes on each side, or until browned. Top it with the stuffing mixture. Roast in the oven, uncovered, for 55 to 65 minutes. The internal temperature should be 150°F and the top stuffing crispy brown. Allow the roast to rest for 15 minutes before carving.

Arista (accent on the *ár*-) is king of the pork roasts in Tuscany. Usually, the roast is simply seasoned and roasted in the oven—plain but mighty! Giusi throws on a small glass of brandy near the end of cooking time.

Ed's favorite pork loin elaborates on the classic. With a sharp knife, he makes a big pocket in a *primo* center-cut loin, and then brines it for 2 hours. Meanwhile, he assembles his *odori*, breadcrumbs, and herbs. His quantities are improvised, but with these ingredients, you can't go wrong. Sometimes he pours on a small glass of *vin santo* near the end of roasting. That's it—the glory of Saturday night dinner with good friends. This debuts with grace at a major feast, too.

We're lucky to have Avignonesi vineyards near Cortona. With the *arista* we like their fabulous DOC Cortona Merlot, Desiderio.

ROASTED VEAL SHANK

SERVES 6

The famous paintings of Piero della Francesca are not the only reason to go to Sansepolcro. Da Ventura, an old-style *trattoria*, serves three meats from a cart: pork with a crunchy crust, a beef stew, and this tasty whole veal shank, *stinco di vitello*. Your butcher may have to order this cut, which is ossobuco left whole. This is our number one house favorite—fall-off-your-chair tasty and so very easy. Our friend Riccardo Baracchi's Ardito, made from syrah and cabernet sauvignon grapes, is a perfect choice for this meltingly tender *vitello*.

- 1 VEAL SHANK, ABOUT 3 POUNDS
- 2 TABLESPOONS EXTRA-VIRGIN OLIVE OIL
- 1 TABLESPOON FRESH THYME LEAVES OR 1½ TEASPOONS DRIED
- 1 TABLESPOON MINCED FRESH ROSEMARY OR 1½ TEASPOONS DRIED
- 4 GARLIC CLOVES, MINCED
- 1 TEASPOON SALT
- 1 TEASPOON PEPPER
- ½ CUP WATER
- ½ CUP WHITE WINE

Preheat the oven to 275°F.

In an 8-quart enameled casserole with a lid, over medium heat, brown the shank all over in the olive oil for about 8 minutes. Remove from the heat. Let it cool enough so that you can pat the herbs, garlic, and seasonings onto the meat. Return it to the pot, cover, and slow-roast for 1½ hours. Gently turn the meat and pour the water over it. Continue to roast for 30 more minutes, and then pour the wine over it. Roast for 1 hour more (3 hours total). The meat will have shrunk away from the bone somewhat and will almost fall off. Let it rest for 10 to 15 minutes. Serve whole on a platter and pull off pieces with a large fork. Serve the pan juices in a separate bowl or douse the veal all at once.

ROLLED VEAL SCALLOPS FILLED *with* ARTICHOKES

SERVES 8

FOR THE FILLING

10	SMALL ARTICHOKES, PRICKLY TOPS CUT OFF
¼	CUP EXTRA-VIRGIN OLIVE OIL
½	RED ONION, MINCED
2	GARLIC CLOVES, MINCED
¾	CUP FRESH BREADCRUMBS, TOASTED
3	TABLESPOONS MASCARPONE
1	EGG, BEATEN

8	VEAL SCALLOPS, ABOUT 2 POUNDS TOTAL
¼	CUP EXTRA-VIRGIN OLIVE OIL
½	CUP ALL-PURPOSE FLOUR, FOR DREDGING
¾	CUP RED WINE
¾	CUP CHICKEN STOCK
1	CUP (8 OUNCES) MASCARPONE

Make the filling. Steam the artichokes until a leaf pulls away easily, 10 to 15 minutes. Remove the artichokes and let them cool. Strip off the outer leaves until you reach the palest green ones. Leave these soft leaves but remove the thistle. Chop the artichokes coarsely.

In a large skillet over low heat, heat the olive oil and sauté the onion and garlic for 2 minutes, then add the artichoke pieces and continue cooking for another 3 to 4 minutes. Stir in the breadcrumbs and cook 2 minutes. Remove from the heat to a medium bowl. When the mixture is cool, add 3 tablespoons of mascarpone and the egg. Stir well.

Have your butcher pound the veal scallops quite thin, or flatten them between layers of plastic wrap, using a meat pounder. Lay out the veal pieces on a work surface and divide the artichoke mixture among them. Spread the filling, roll up each scallop, and tie with string.

Over medium heat, add the oil to the skillet. Pat the veal rolls with flour and sauté them for about 5 minutes, turning once. When browned, test for doneness by cutting into the veal. It should have a streak of pink inside. Remove the veal rolls to a plate and cover them.

Add the wine and chicken stock to the pan and boil vigorously for 5 minutes, or until reduced by half. Remove from the heat, and stir in the 1 cup mascarpone, allowing it to melt gently into the liquid. Spoon some sauce on top and proceed to the table.

Artichokes add architectural emphasis to a garden. The artichokes that we forget to pick become dry and then transform into brilliant blue thistles, nice to mix with wildflowers.

In Italian, veal scallops that are filled and rolled are said to resemble *uccellini*, little birds. Serve the veal "birds" whole, or for a nicer presentation, remove the strings, slice each rolled scallop into 1½-inch-thick pieces, and arrange in a fan shape on individual plates. For this recipe, open a full-bodied merlot, perhaps Vignalta's Colli Euganei Rosso Gemola (with 25 percent Cabernet Franc), a wine from the area southwest of Venice, near where the fourteenth-century poet Petrarch lived at the end of his life. I think a verse of his poetry melted into the grapes.

LITTLE VEAL MEATBALLS
with ARTICHOKES *and* CHERRY TOMATOES

SERVES 4

Spring causes artichoke madness all over Italy, especially in Rome. As a break from their best-loved *carciofi alla giudia* (a Roman legacy from the Jewish ghetto), I ordered *polpettine* one April night, when dining outside at Matricianella, a small *trattoria* near Piazza San Lorenzo in Lucina. I've been making it ever since. When Ed grills slabs of crusty polenta, as they did that night in Rome, we consider this to be the perfect Sunday-night supper—quick, one pan, delicious. When forming the *polpettine*, flatten each one so that it looks like a slightly crushed Ping-Pong ball.

2	LARGE SLICES OF RUSTIC BREAD
1	CUP WHOLE MILK
½	TEASPOON SALT
½	TEASPOON PEPPER
	A FEW GRATINGS OF NUTMEG
4	TABLESPOONS MINCED FLAT-LEAF PARSLEY
3	GARLIC CLOVES, MINCED
1	EGG
1	POUND GROUND VEAL
½	CUP (2 OUNCES) GRATED PARMIGIANO-REGGIANO
3	TABLESPOONS EXTRA-VIRGIN OLIVE OIL
6	ARTICHOKE HEARTS, STEAMED AND QUARTERED, OR 1 14-OUNCE CAN WATER-PACKED ARTICHOKE HEARTS
25	CHERRY TOMATOES
¼	CUP WHITE WINE
4	TABLESPOONS TOMATO SAUCE (PAGE 21)
1	TABLESPOON FRESH THYME OR 1½ TEASPOONS DRIED

In a large bowl, soak the bread in the milk, and then break apart the bread with two forks. Add the salt, pepper, nutmeg, parsley, and garlic. Blend well. Stir in the egg, then the veal and Parmigiano, and combine well.

Heat the olive oil in a 14-inch skillet over medium heat. With damp hands, roll the mixture into small balls, flatten slightly, add to the pan, and brown them 3 minutes on each side, or until almost cooked through. Remove to a large bowl.

Add the artichokes, tomatoes, wine, tomato sauce, and thyme to the pan. Toss to combine. Turn the heat to high for a minute, and then lower it immediately. Return the meatballs to the pan, mixing them in with a wide spatula. Cook on medium for about 3 minutes, or until the tomatoes are plumped.

SHORT RIBS, TUSCAN STYLE

SERVES 6

5	POUNDS BEEF SHORT RIBS, APPROXIMATELY ¾ POUND EACH
1	CUP ALL-PURPOSE FLOUR, FOR DREDGING
1½	TEASPOONS SALT
1	TEASPOON PEPPER
7	TABLESPOONS EXTRA-VIRGIN OLIVE OIL
1	YELLOW ONION, CHOPPED
2	CARROTS, CHOPPED
2	CELERY STALKS, CHOPPED
3	GARLIC CLOVES, MINCED
½	BOTTLE RED WINE
16	TOMATOES OR 2 28-OUNCE CANS WHOLE TOMATOES, CHOPPED
10	SPRIGS OF THYME
2	CUPS BEEF STOCK

The Tuscan way with oven-cooked ribs—low and slow—results in deep flavor and fall-off-the-bone meat. We always choose this during the olive harvest and serve the ribs with Polenta Parmigiana to family and friends who pick olives with us. They've all earned a rich and savory feast and lots of big-mouthed wine, such as Baracchi's Smeriglio Syrah.

Preheat the oven to 325°F.

In a paper bag, dredge the ribs in the flour and season with the salt and pepper. Over medium heat, place 5 tablespoons of the olive oil in an 8-quart enameled casserole with a lid. Brown the ribs on all sides, in batches if necessary, 7 or 8 minutes. Remove to a plate.

Add the remaining 2 tablespoons of the olive oil, the onion, carrots, celery, and garlic to the casserole, and sauté for 3 minutes over medium-low heat, until the vegetables are coated with oil and beginning to soften. Add the wine, turn the heat up to high, and cook for 2 to 3 minutes. Stir in the tomatoes and their juice. Add the ribs, the thyme, and stock. Bring the pot back to a boil, cover, and transfer to the oven. Cook for 2 hours or until the meat is meltingly tender.

OSSOBUCO

SERVES 4

Mario Ponticelli owns Trattoria Etrusca, in Cortona—a few tables inside and a few tables outside. We've eaten what he's served, either way. This is his ossobuco. To hers, my friend Franca adds green olives. Italians prize the marrow as much as the meat. I love the dash of fresh green taste that gremolata adds. Choose big, meaty *ossibuchi*.

The ossobuco calls for a splurge—Castiglione Vietti, DOCG, Barolo.

4 PIECES OSSOBUCO, ABOUT 9 OUNCES EACH, TIED WITH KITCHEN TWINE
1 TEASPOON SALT
½ TEASPOON PEPPER
¼ CUP EXTRA-VIRGIN OLIVE OIL
1 YELLOW ONION, FINELY CHOPPED
1 CARROT, FINELY CHOPPED
1 CELERY STALK, FINELY CHOPPED
3 GARLIC CLOVES, MINCED
8 TOMATOES OR 1 28-OUNCE CAN WHOLE TOMATOES, JUICE INCLUDED, CHOPPED
½ TEASPOON FRESH THYME LEAVES OR ¼ TEASPOON DRIED
½ TEASPOON FRESH OREGANO LEAVES OR ¼ TEASPOON DRIED

FOR THE GREMOLATA
1 HANDFUL OF FLAT-LEAF PARSLEY, CHOPPED
ZEST OF 1 LEMON
ZEST OF 1 ORANGE
5 GARLIC CLOVES, MINCED

Preheat the oven to 350°F.

Season both sides of the ossobuco with the salt and pepper. In an 8-quart, enameled casserole with a lid, over medium-high heat, brown the meat in 3 tablespoons of the olive oil, about 3 minutes per side. Remove the meat, turn the heat to medium low, and add the remaining 1 tablespoon olive oil, the onion, carrot, and celery. Cook for 5 minutes, stirring occasionally. Stir in the garlic, tomatoes, thyme, and oregano. Add the ossobuco, cover, and transfer to the oven. Bake for 1½ hours or until the meat is tender—actually falling off the bone.

In a small bowl, mix the parsley, lemon and orange zests, and garlic to make the gremolata. Top the ossobuco with gremolata and serve.

Placido's STEAK

SERVES 1 OR 2

- 1 BIG, THICK T-BONE STEAK
- 3 TABLESPOONS EXTRA-VIRGIN OLIVE OIL
- 1/2 TEASPOON SALT, OR TO TASTE
- 1/2 TEASPOON PEPPER, OR TO TASTE
- 1/2 TEASPOON FRESH ROSEMARY, PLUS WANDS FOR BASTING
- 1 GARLIC CLOVE, MINCED (OPTIONAL—PLARI DOES NOT USE IT)

Heat the grill. Cut gashes in the strip of fat on the outside of the steak so that it doesn't curl up in the heat. In a shallow pan (large enough to hold the steak), combine the olive oil, salt, pepper, rosemary, and garlic.

Place the steak on the hot grill. Do not touch it for at least 2 minutes. Turn over and cook for another 2 minutes. While the steak is grilling, baste it with a rosemary wand dipped in the olive oil bath. Remove the steak from the grill and quickly dip in the oil bath on both sides, sprinkling on more salt and pepper. Serve warm and garnish with the rosemary wands.

Whether he's cooking porcini, slabs of pancetta, or pigeons, Placido remains perfectly at ease. When he mans several grills at the annual Ferragosto party, Lina sings as he's enveloped in smoke, and everyone dances on the terrace. We all arrive with our steaks in hand and turn them over to the *maestro.*

First, we've been to Claudio's *macelleria* and have asked for the same kind of steak that Plari buys for himself. Behind the counter, Antonella selects a hefty hunk and whacks off excess fat. We walk out with gargantuan steaks from those huge white cows called *Chianina,* for the Val di Chiana where they're raised.

While a steak is on the grill, Plari bastes it with a wand of rosemary dipped in oil. Tuscans like their steak *al sangue,* bloody, so grilling time here is approximate. After the steak is lifted from its oil bath, dip slices of bread into the oil, and grill them for quick *bruschette.*

"FINGER-BURNER" LAMB CHOPS

SERVES 4

2	TABLESPOONS EXTRA-VIRGIN OLIVE OIL
1/3	CUP RED WINE
1	TABLESPOON FRESH THYME LEAVES OR 1½ TEASPOONS DRIED
1	TEASPOON SALT
1	TEASPOON PEPPER
16	LAMB LOIN CHOPS, FROM 2 RACKS OF LAMB

In a deep glass container with a lid, mix the olive oil, wine, thyme, salt, and pepper. Add the chops and shake well. Cover and refrigerate for 5 hours, shaking once in a while.

Heat a grill, if using. Remove the chops and discard the marinade. Grill the chops over a hot fire or a strong flame, about a minute or so on each side. They should be well browned on both sides and pink inside. (If you're using a stovetop grill pan, over medium-high heat, cook the chops for 2 minutes on each side—the meat will be pink inside, and at 2½ minutes, slightly pink.) Cut into a chop to check for how you like it.

Serve while finger-burning hot!

The name "finger-burners," *scottaditi,* makes sense when you pick up these delectable small chops right off the grill. They also can be pan-roasted quickly over high heat in the kitchen. To save time, ask the butcher to cut the racks into individual chops.

I suggest Lisini's Rosso di Montalcino with the *scottaditi.*

THE PECORINO OF PIENZA

The drive from Cortona to Montepulciano, especially if you detour to sublime Monte-chiello, is one of the most evocative in Tuscany. Then, toward Pienza, the terraced hillsides of grapes give way to a different landscape, where wheat fields stretch as far as the eye can see. At harvest the round bales stud the golden, rolling hills. Goaded by Sardinian shepherds, sheep move in clumps, the lambs cavorting outside the herd. Looking at a black lamb in the wildflowers, I never think *scottaditi,* or slow-roasted leg of lamb, but, as we drive by, I often say, "Pecorino in the making," for this is prime territory for that revered ewe-milk cheese. Fresh and creamy or *semi-stagionata* (aged three or four months) or *stagionata* (aged about a year, until hard and flaky like Parmigiano)—all are locally loved. Cheese shops line the main street of the noble renaissance town of Pienza. You can taste pecorinos wrapped in walnut leaves or straw, dusted with ashes, coated with red pepper or concentrated tomato paste, studded with truffles, drenched in wine, or just plain. They've been aged on shelves in a cantina, or in terracotta vats, or in *fosse,* caves or pits. Vacuum-wrapped, the cheeses travel home happily, to be brought out with a glass of something essentially Tuscan on an evening when you're reliving the drive through the blissful Tuscan countryside.

ROAST LEG *of* LAMB *with* HERBS *and* PANCETTA

SERVES 8

1	BONELESS LEG OF LAMB, ABOUT 4 POUNDS
1/4	POUND PANCETTA OR BACON, FINELY CHOPPED
8 TO 10	FRESH SAGE LEAVES, TORN
1	TABLESPOON MINCED FRESH ROSEMARY OR
	1 1/2 TEASPOONS DRIED
	EXTRA-VIRGIN OLIVE OIL
1	TEASPOON SALT
1/2	TEASPOON PEPPER
6	TABLESPOONS (3/4 STICK) UNSALTED BUTTER
4	GARLIC CLOVES, CHOPPED
1/2	CUP WHITE WINE VINEGAR
1/2	CUP WHITE WINE
	FRESH MINT SPRIGS OR ROSEMARY WANDS

The butcher can prepare the meat for you. All you do is make gashes for herbs and pancetta, then slide it into the oven. While the lamb cooks, prepare *involtini di melanzane* (page 166). Eggplant is the classic Mediterranean combination with lamb. You can add some potatoes and carrots that have been tossed with olive oil to the lamb for the last hour of cooking, basting them a couple of times. Of the many roast lambs I have tried, this one is divine—flavorful savory juices and succulent tender lamb.

The Cortona syrah, Tenimento d'Alessandro, Il Bosco, will be perfection with the lamb.

Preheat the oven to 350°F.

Using a sharp knife, cut 2-inch slits into the lamb. In a small bowl, mix the pancetta with most of the sage and rosemary. Stuff this into the slits and into any folds or crevices. Brush the lamb with olive oil, season with the salt and pepper, and place it in a roasting pan with the butter, garlic, and any remaining stuffing mixture.

Heat the vinegar and white wine to a boil in a small saucepan. Stir and pour into the roasting pan.

Roast the lamb for 1 1/2 hours for rare (140°F internal temperature) or 2 hours for pink (165°F). Turn the lamb over after 45 minutes. During the roasting, moisten occasionally with the sauce from the bottom of the pan. Let it rest for 10 to 15 minutes before carving.

Garnish with the mint or rosemary.

BEEF TENDERLOIN *with* BALSAMIC VINEGAR

SERVES 6

FOR THE SAUCE

4	SHALLOTS, MINCED
2	TABLESPOONS EXTRA-VIRGIN OLIVE OIL
2	GARLIC CLOVES, MINCED
½	TEASPOON SALT
¼	TEASPOON PEPPER
½	CUP BALSAMIC VINEGAR
½	CUP RED WINE
1	BAY LEAF
6	6-OUNCE FILETS OF BEEF TENDERLOIN (2¼-POUND TENDERLOIN CUT INTO 6 PIECES)
½	TEASPOON SALT
¼	TEASPOON PEPPER
2	TABLESPOONS EXTRA-VIRGIN OLIVE OIL

The night before my daughter flies out of Florence, she always wants her favorite steak at Ristorante Parione, on the street of the same name. The chef told Ed not to use prized balsamic for this, but to use one "good enough."

With this dish, my daughter recommends Amarone, her favorite wine. Some are stratospheric in price. Try the Corte Sant'Alda Amarone della Valpolicella.

Make the sauce. In a small pan over medium heat, sauté the shallots in the olive oil for 3 minutes. Add the garlic, salt, and pepper in the last minute. Stir in the balsamic vinegar, red wine, and bay leaf and bring to a boil. Reduce to a simmer and cook for about 10 minutes, until the vinegar-wine sauce is concentrated and thickened.

Season the tenderloins with the remaining salt and pepper. In a large skillet over medium-high heat, sauté the tenderloins in the olive oil 2 minutes on each side for *al sangue,* rare.

Remove the bay leaf from the balsamic sauce and spoon it over the filets of beef.

RICH POLENTA PARMIGIANA
with FUNGHI PORCINI

  2 CUPS POLENTA
  3 CUPS COLD WATER
3 TO 4 CUPS WATER, FOR BOILING
  1 TABLESPOON SALT
  1 TABLESPOON PEPPER
  ½ CUP (1 STICK) UNSALTED BUTTER
  1 CUP (4 OUNCES) GRATED PARMIGIANO-REGGIANO

FOR THE PORCINI SAUCE

  5 GARLIC CLOVES, MINCED
  2 TABLESPOONS EXTRA-VIRGIN OLIVE OIL
  1 TABLESPOON FRESH THYME LEAVES OR
    1½ TEASPOONS DRIED
  1 TABLESPOON MINCED FRESH ROSEMARY OR
    1½ TEASPOONS DRIED
  1 CUP TOMATO SAUCE (PAGE 21; ⅓ RECIPE)
  1 TEASPOON SALT
  1 TEASPOON PEPPER
  2 OUNCES DRIED PORCINI, RECONSTITUTED
    (SEE PAGE 28)

Preheat the oven to 300°F.

Soak the polenta in the cold water for 10 minutes. In a stockpot, bring 3 cups of water to a boil and stir in the soaked polenta. Let it come to a boil again, then turn down the heat immediately and stir for 15 minutes over gentle heat that is strong enough to keep slow, big bubbles plopping to the surface. Stir in the salt and pepper, butter, and Parmigiano. When the butter has melted, add the last cup of water if the polenta is too thick. Remove from the heat. Stir well and pour polenta into a large buttered baking dish. Bake for about 15 minutes to finish the cooking.

Make the sauce. In a medium saucepan over low heat, cook the garlic in the olive oil for 1 minute. Add the thyme, rosemary, tomato sauce, salt, and pepper. Remove the mushrooms from the water and squeeze dry but don't chop them. Strain the mushroom water through cheese-cloth and add 1 cup of it to the tomato mixture. Add the mushrooms and raise the heat to a simmer until thick and savory, about 20 minutes.

Spoon the sauce over the polenta.

This is an extravagant take on traditional Italian polenta. I've served this amplified version to Italians and they've loved it.

This recipe calls for only 2 ounces of dried porcini. A little bit holds a lot of flavor. Instead of dried porcini, you can use 2 cups of any wild mushrooms.

If fresh porcini are available, chop two or three good-sized ones into large dice and sauté them with the garlic. Instead of the mushroom water listed in the recipe, use 1 cup of white wine quickly brought to a boil, then added to the tomato mixture. Spoon this sauce over the polenta or serve it as a pasta sauce.

Fresh porcini are at their finest simply brushed with olive oil and grilled, a dish that is as substantial as steak.

Leftover polenta is *delizioso* when cubed, fried, and served as croutons on salad.

POLENTA *with* SAUSAGE *and* FONTINA

SERVES 8

2 CUPS COLD WATER
4 CUPS WATER, FOR BOILING
2 CUPS POLENTA
1 TEASPOON SALT
1/2 CUP GRATED PARMIGIANO-REGGIANO
   EXTRA-VIRGIN OLIVE OIL, FOR THE PAN
6 ITALIAN SAUSAGES, COOKED AND SLICED, PAN JUICES
   RESERVED
1/2 CUP WALNUTS, CHOPPED AND TOASTED
16 OUNCES THINLY SLICED FONTINA
   SALT AND PEPPER TO TASTE

In winter, the local fresh pasta shop sells polenta with chopped walnuts, a simple but interesting accompaniment to roasts or chicken. With the addition of sausages and a grand salad, a down-home meal is ready, *pronto*. Use either this traditional polenta or the rich version (page 137). Regular cornmeal is ground too fine; choose an Italian polenta, which will have a medium-coarse texture.

Soak the polenta in the cold water for 10 minutes. In a stockpot, bring 4 cups of water to a boil. Add the soaked polenta to the pot, stirring well, then lower the heat to a simmer. Add the salt and keep stirring. Big bubbles will rise to the top and pop. As the polenta thickens and absorbs the water, continue adding water. Take care to stir deeply so the polenta doesn't stick. After 20 minutes, stir in the Parmigiano. The texture should be thick and creamy. If it seems dense, don't hesitate to add additional water; some grinds are more absorbent.

Preheat the oven to 300°F. Oil a 9 x 13-inch baking dish.

Mix the sausage slices and walnuts into the polenta. The consistency should be that of a creamy cake batter. Pour half of the polenta into the baking dish. Arrange the fontina slices over the polenta. Season with salt and pepper. Pour on the rest of the polenta, then add any pan juices from the sausages. Bake for 20 minutes to heat through and melt the cheese.

PASTA FRITTATA

1	YELLOW ONION, FINELY CHOPPED
2	TABLESPOONS EXTRA-VIRGIN OLIVE OIL
1/4	CUP WHOLE MILK
6	EGGS, BEATEN
1	CUP LEFTOVER PASTA
1/2	TEASPOON SALT
1/2	TEASPOON PEPPER
1/2	CUP (2 OUNCES) GRATED PARMIGIANO-REGGIANO
1	LARGE TOMATO, SLICED
1	HANDFUL OF FLAT-LEAF PARSLEY, CHOPPED

Preheat the broiler. In a 10-inch skillet over medium heat, sauté the onion in the oil until translucent, about 2 minutes. In a bowl, beat the milk into the eggs. Stir the pasta, seasonings, and cheese into the eggs, and pour into the pan. Arrange the tomato slices on top of the egg mixture, and cook over medium-low heat until semi-set, about 8 minutes. Sprinkle with parsley. Run the frittata under the broiler for 1 minute. Keep an eye on it so the top doesn't scorch.

Frittatas are enormously popular in Tuscany. Not that you encounter them on menus—they show up more on the kitchen table, when the family is watching a soccer game, or when someone has found a handful of wild asparagus, or when there's a little leftover pasta and can't we do something with it?

Use a cast-iron skillet and take it right to the table. Serve with tomato sauce (page 21).

Giusi's EGGPLANT PARMIGIANA

2	MEDIUM EGGPLANTS, SLICED 1/4 INCH THICK
1/3	CUP EXTRA-VIRGIN OLIVE OIL
1	TEASPOON SALT, OR TO TASTE
3	CUPS TOMATO SAUCE (PAGE 21)
1	HANDFUL OF BASIL LEAVES, TORN
1	CUP (4 OUNCES) GRATED PARMIGIANO-REGGIANO
2	CUPS (8 OUNCES) SHREDDED MOZZARELLA

Ed went on a quest to duplicate, exactly, the eggplant Parmigiana Giusi sometimes brings over as a surprise.

Preheat the oven to 350°F. Place the eggplant slices on 2 parchment-lined sheet pans. Brush them with the olive oil, salt them, and roast for 10 to 12 minutes, until fork tender. Spoon some tomato sauce into the bottom of a 9 x 13-inch baking dish. Add one-third of the eggplant, then a layer of tomato sauce, a few basil leaves, a third of the Parmigiano, and a third of the mozzarella. Add another two layers of eggplant, sauce, basil, and cheeses, finishing with mozzarella on top. Bake for 35 minutes, or until the top is browned and bubbling.

FRITTO MISTO

The most important ingredient in *fritto misto* is the person selling the fish. Fresh is the word for all fish, of course. Ask for a variety of seafood—all cleaned and ready to go. Small fish should have their innards removed but otherwise be left whole. Fish such as sole and cod should be filleted and cut into 3-inch chunks.

Fritto misto is surprisingly light because it's fried quickly. You might want to fry a few zucchini, potato sticks, and carrots, too. As an antipasto, this serves 10 to 12.

A crisp sauvignon blanc, such as Venica & Venica's Ronco de Cerò, pairs well.

SERVES 6

- 5 CUPS PEANUT OR SUNFLOWER OIL, FOR FRYING
- 1 CUP ALL-PURPOSE FLOUR
- 1 TEASPOON SALT
- 1 TEASPOON PEPPER
- 4 POUNDS MIXED SEAFOOD (SQUID, SCALLOPS, SHRIMP, PRAWNS, FISH), CLEANED AND SHELLED OR FILLETED
  LEMON WEDGES

In a 12-inch skillet, heat the oil to 350°F.

In a large bowl, combine the flour, salt, and pepper. Dredge the seafood, shaking off any excess flour. Fry in batches until crisp and golden, about 30 seconds per side for the shrimp and a few seconds less for the scallops. Depending on the size of the chunks of fish, they will take about a minute. Drain on paper towels. Serve immediately with lemon wedges.

SEA BASS *in a* SALT CRUST

If you happen to go to the Tuscan coast, locate the tiny town of Bibbona, then search for the pine forest and the stretch of beach where the restaurant La Pineta is located. Maybe it looks like a beach shack, but inside you find a digni-fied elegant dining room presided over by owner Luciano Zazzeri and his twin sons. You're seated so close to the sea that a wave could roll into your lap. The catch of the day came out of these waters just this morning. Luciano used to be a fisherman, but now that he has all the guidebooks raving, he leaves the sea to his friends and cousins in Cecina.

Baking a fish in salt crust is about as much fun as you can have in the kitchen. Don't expect a salty fish—the briny crust seals in juices and only slightly penetrates. If sustainable sea bass isn't available, try red snapper.

Bring to the table a Ronchi di Manzano, a Friulano white.

SERVES 6 TO 8

I	LARGE SEA BASS, 3½ TO 4 POUNDS, OR 2 TWO-POUND FISH, CLEANED AND PREPARED FOR COOKING
I	LEMON, THINLY SLICED
	A FEW SPRIGS OF THYME, PLUS A TEASPOON OR SO OF LEAVES
3 OR 4	FRESH ROSEMARY WANDS
	JUICE OF 2 LEMONS
5	TABLESPOONS EXTRA-VIRGIN OLIVE OIL
½	TEASPOON PEPPER
I	HANDFUL OF FLAT-LEAF PARSLEY, CHOPPED
3 TO 5	POUNDS COARSE SALT
½	CUP ALL-PURPOSE FLOUR
2	EGG WHITES

Preheat the oven to 400°F.

Dry the fish well and stuff the inside with slices of lemon, rose-mary, and a few sprigs of thyme. In a small bowl, mix the lemon juice with the olive oil and brush the fish all over, keeping half of the oil mixture for later. Season the fish on both sides with the pepper and half of the parsley and thyme leaves. To the remaining olive oil and lemon mixture, add the rest of the thyme and parsley.

Layer the bottom of a baking dish large enough for the fish with an inch of salt. Place the fish on top, then mix the rest of the salt with the flour, egg whites, and just enough water to make a snowy moist mixture. Spread this over the fish, completely covering and smooth-ing it with a knife.

Bake for 40 minutes, or until the salt looks toasted. Present the fish at the table, cracking or sawing into the hard crust, just for the fun of the display, then take it back to the kitchen. In a small pan over low heat, warm the reserved olive oil and lemon mixture. Remove the salt from the fish and discard it, then peel away the skin. Take off the top layer of the fish, extract the bone, and remove the rest to a platter for serving. Pour on the warm sauce. Serve immediately.

FISHERMAN'S FISH *for* LUNCH

SERVES 1

- EXTRA-VIRGIN OLIVE OIL, FOR A SKILLET THAT FITS THE FISH FILLET
- 2 GARLIC CLOVES, CRUSHED WITH A KNIFE BLADE
- SALT TO TASTE
- 1 FISH FILLET
- SPLASH OF WHITE WINE
- 5 CHERRY TOMATOES
- SOME FLAT-LEAF PARSLEY, CHOPPED

Heat the oil in the skillet over medium-low heat and then add the garlic. Let the garlic infuse the oil for 2 minutes, then remove the cloves. Salt the fish lightly, turn up the heat to medium, and place the fish in the skillet. Add the splash of wine. Cover the skillet and cook until the fish is firm and flaky, about 2 minutes. Add the tomatoes and continue cooking for 1 or 2 minutes more, or longer, depending on the thickness of the fish. Don't turn it during cooking. Remove from the heat, sprinkle with parsley, and serve.

After a lunch at La Pineta, on the beach in Bibbona, we were interested in seeing where the catch came from. Chef/owner Luciano Zazzeri directed us to a riverside dock in Cecina, where he once plied his boat and where fourteen of his friends and cousins still dock. Early the next day we arrived as the men were unloading their nets. Papero Di Donato showed us his catch and told us how he fillets and prepares fish. His daily lunch could not be simpler. "Where's the best place to eat in Cecina?" I asked him. He answered, "My house."

I wonder if Papero would allow a variation, which we were served the next day at a seaside restaurant farther down the coast: to the fish—we had *spigola*, sea bass—the cook added some cubed boiled potatoes and a few olives, along with the cherry tomatoes. But here is Papero's daily *pranzo*.

Use what's fresh— sole, flounder, perch, or salmon.

ROLLED SOLE *with* FENNEL *and* CITRUS

Every summer we harvest the wild fennel flowers, dry them, and keep them all year to sprinkle on oven-roasted potatoes. Fennel has many virtues. Baked, it couldn't be better. You simply cut three or four fennel bulbs into eighths, steam them until barely tender, spread them in a well-oiled baking dish, drizzle with more olive oil, and add a sprinkling of Parmigiano. Then, run the dish into the oven for 20 minutes at 350°F. I first discovered a version of this in the Florence airport restaurant!

A salad of thinly sliced fennel, minced shallot, blood orange sections, and crisp pungent lettuces lightens a dinner with a substantial meat course. Fennel also marries well with fish, as we see here.

Ever since we visited the Villa Matilde vineyard north of Naples, we've poured their wines. Their DOCG Greco di Tufo seems to hold a few rays of that southern sun.

1 FENNEL BULB, TOUGH OUTER PARTS DISCARDED, DICED
3 TABLESPOONS EXTRA-VIRGIN OLIVE OIL
1 TEASPOON FENNEL FLOWERS OR CRUSHED FENNEL SEEDS
1 GARLIC CLOVE, MINCED
1 ORANGE, PEELED, SECTIONED, AND DICED
JUICE AND ZEST OF 1 ORANGE AND 1 LEMON
1 CUP FRESH BREADCRUMBS, TOASTED
6 FILLETS OF SOLE
½ CUP WHITE WINE
2 TABLESPOONS FENNEL FRONDS OR FLAT-LEAF PARSLEY, CHOPPED

Preheat the oven to 350°F.

In a medium skillet over medium-low heat, sauté the diced fennel in 1 tablespoon of the olive oil until barely tender, about 3 minutes. Stir in the fennel flowers or seeds, then the garlic, just for a final minute. Stir in the orange sections, the citrus zest (reserving some for garnish), and ⅔ cup of the breadcrumbs. Remove from the stove.

Top each fish fillet with a layer of the fennel mixture. Gently roll up the fillets and secure them with toothpicks. Arrange the rolls in a 6 x 9-inch baking dish. Drizzle with the remaining 2 tablespoons olive oil and ¼ cup of the wine, and sprinkle with the remaining breadcrumbs. Bake uncovered for 20 minutes or until the sole has white edges and the crumbs are browned.

In a small saucepan, combine the juices of the lemon and orange along with the remaining ¼ cup wine. Bring to a boil, then lower the heat to medium and let the sauce reduce for 10 minutes.

Remove the fish to a platter and stir the juices from the baking dish into the citrus juice mixture. Spoon the sauce on top of the fish and garnish with the remaining zests and the fennel fronds.

BRODETTO

SERVES 6

2	SHALLOTS, MINCED
¼	CUP EXTRA-VIRGIN OLIVE OIL
4	GARLIC CLOVES, MINCED
4 TO 5	SAFFRON THREADS, SOAKED FOR I HOUR IN I TABLESPOON TEPID WATER
I	TEASPOON SALT
½	TEASPOON PEPPER
25	CHERRY TOMATOES, HALVED
2	CUPS WHITE WINE
½	POUND COD FILLET, CUT INTO I-INCH PIECES
I	POUND SHRIMP, PEELED AND CLEANED
8	OUNCES SMALL SEA SCALLOPS
8	OUNCES FLOUNDER FILLET, CUT INTO I-INCH PIECES
I	HANDFUL OF FLAT-LEAF PARSLEY, CHOPPED

In a large saucepan over medium-low heat, soften the shallots in the olive oil for 2 or 3 minutes, and then stir in the garlic, saffron, saffron water, salt, pepper, and tomatoes. Continue cooking for 5 more minutes. Add the wine and bring to a boil, and immediately lower the heat to a simmer for 5 more minutes, stirring occasionally, until well blended.

Raise the heat to medium and add the cod, which takes a little longer than the other seafood. Cook for 3 minutes, turning once, and then add the shrimp, scallops, and flounder. Cover, reduce the heat to low, and cook for 15 minutes, or until all the seafood is done. Add the parsley just before serving.

If you look on a topographical map of Italy, you'll see that the Apennines form a sturdy and well-articulated spine, splitting the country in two. On the eastern side, the mountains slope to wide, fertile plains that end in the Tyrrhenian, the Tuscan part of the Mediterranean Sea. There's no such landscape on the western side of the Apennines, where mountains and sea have a more intimate relationship. Up and down the Adriatic coast, you'll find that everyone who has a stockpot has a recipe for *brodetto*.

For any fish stew, buy what's fresh. If the recipe calls for flounder and there's no flounder and the hake looks good, then buy hake. Traditionally, cooks use thirteen different kinds of seafood.

Serve the *brodetto* in a bowl over *bruschetta* or spaghetti. Pour a red, such as Dei's Rosso di Montalcino, or a spirited white, such as Panizzi's Vernaccia di San Gimignano.

Franca's SEA BASS

- ¼ CUP ALL-PURPOSE FLOUR
- 1 TEASPOON SALT
- ½ TEASPOON PEPPER
- 1½ POUNDS SEA BASS, SNAPPER, AMBERJACK, OR OTHER FIRM WHITE FISH FILLET, CUT INTO 2- TO 3-INCH CHUNKS
- 4 TO 6 TABLESPOONS EXTRA-VIRGIN OLIVE OIL
- 1 YELLOW OR RED ONION, VERY THINLY SLICED
- 3 TABLESPOONS BALSAMIC OR RED WINE VINEGAR
- 3 GARLIC CLOVES, THINLY SLICED
- 4 TO 5 SAFFRON THREADS, SOAKED FOR 1 HOUR IN 1 TABLESPOON TEPID WATER
- 1 FENNEL BULB, THINLY SLICED AND LIGHTLY BLANCHED
- 2 TABLESPOONS RAISINS
- 5 DRIED APRICOTS, SLICED
- ½ CUP ALMONDS OR HAZELNUTS, HALVED AND TOASTED
- ½ CUP MIXED GREEN AND BLACK OLIVES
- 3 BAY LEAVES

Combine the flour with the salt and pepper in a large bowl, and lightly dredge the pieces of fish. In a large skillet, over medium heat, brown the fish in 2 tablespoons of the olive oil, about 2 minutes per side or until barely cooked through. Add a little more oil if needed. Remove and drain the fish on paper towels.

Add the remaining 2 or 3 tablespoons of olive oil to the same pan, and adjust the heat to low. Cook the onion until soft and starting to color, about 2 minutes. Stir in the vinegar, garlic, saffron, and saffron water. Remove from the heat.

Arrange the fish in a large glass baking dish. Add the fennel slices, raisins, apricots, nuts, olives, and bay leaves. Pour the hot vinegar and onion mixture over everything, cover tightly, and refrigerate for at least 12 hours, turning the fish a couple of times.

This recipe comes from Franca Dotti, a Milanese who now runs The Catering Company of Chapel Hill, North Carolina. Franca first sent it to Ed with this note: *"Non ti mando le quantità, perchè, da buona italiana, faccio tutto ad occhio,"* which means, "I didn't send you the amounts because, as a good Italian, I do it all by eye."

Start this early in the morning to serve at night. Serve it right out of the fridge in summer or reheat during colder months.

Vietti Roero Arneis from Piemonte is a great wine partner here. The grape variety *arneis* means "little rascal," a feisty partner to this exotic fish.

PRAWNS *and* CHERRY TOMATOES *with* PURÉE *of* CANNELLINI

Villa La Massa, one of the premier hotels in Italy, is located just outside Florence. Head chef Andrea Quagliarella gave me this recipe. The unusual pairing reminds me of the Southern classic, shrimp and grits.

With this, try the well-structured and delightful sauvignon from Sanct Valentin.

SERVES 6

20	LARGE PRAWNS, SHELLED
20	MEDIUM SHRIMP, SHELLED
1/4	CUP EXTRA-VIRGIN OLIVE OIL
1	TEASPOON SALT
6	CHERRY TOMATOES, QUARTERED
8 TO 10	SPRIGS OF FRESH THYME
1	POUND CANNELLINI BEANS, COOKED AND WELL SEASONED (PAGE 24), 1/2 CUP OF COOKING WATER RESERVED PEPPER TO TASTE

In a medium skillet over medium heat, sauté the prawns and shrimp in 2 tablespoons of the olive oil for 2 to 3 minutes or until pink. Remove from the heat and season with the salt.

In a small bowl, mix the tomatoes with 1 tablespoon of the olive oil and most of the thyme. Purée the beans with enough cooking water (up to 1/2 cup) to form a light cream. Pour it into soup plates. Add the prawns, shrimp, and tomatoes. Drizzle the plates with the remaining 1 tablespoon olive oil and grind some pepper on top. Garnish with remaining thyme.

Frances's SUMMER SHRIMP SALAD

SERVES 6 TO 8

1½ POUNDS MEDIUM SHRIMP, PEELED AND CLEANED
2   TABLESPOONS EXTRA-VIRGIN OLIVE OIL
½   GARLIC CLOVE, MINCED

FOR THE MARINADE
¼   CUP TARRAGON VINEGAR
1   CUP EXTRA-VIRGIN OLIVE OIL
1   TABLESPOON GOOD MUSTARD
2   GARLIC CLOVES, MINCED
1   TEASPOON SALT
½   TEASPOON PEPPER
¼   TEASPOON PAPRIKA
    SPLASH OF HOT SAUCE
    SPRIGS OF THYME
1   GREEN BELL PEPPER, CHOPPED
3   SHALLOTS, MINCED
2   CELERY STALKS, FINELY CHOPPED

    ENOUGH ARUGULA TO FILL A PLATTER
1   TABLESPOON EXTRA-VIRGIN OLIVE OIL
    AVOCADO AND MANGO, SLICED, FOR GARNISH
    LEMON WEDGES
1   HANDFUL OF FLAT-LEAF PARSLEY, CHOPPED

This recipe travels happily between my kitchens in Tuscany and in North Carolina. Any summer table definitely will be enlivened by its presence. I prefer wild-caught shrimp. For maximum flavor, let the shrimp marinate overnight in the fridge.

In a 12-inch skillet, over medium heat, sauté the shrimp in the olive oil and garlic for about 3 minutes, turning once, until no longer gray—sunrise pink!

Mix everything for the marinade in a large glass container. Add the shrimp. Cover, shake, and marinate the mixture in the fridge up to 24 hours, turning over the container now and then.

Remove the shrimp from the marinade and arrange them on a platter of arugula that has been moistened with the olive oil. Garnish as you like, with avocado and mango (both of which have been moistened with a little of the marinade) and wedges of lemon. Scatter the parsley over the salad and serve.

CONTORNI

"Do you have the beans of Sant'Anna?"

"No, they were in season *last* week." Roberto points to the fresh cannellini. "These are ready now. From all over—Roma, Milano—they come to Tuscany for these beans." I know the cannellini. Simply dressed with oil, sage, salt, and a lot of pepper, they have restorative powers beyond all other beans. I've seen Ed eat them for breakfast. They are Tuscan comfort food.

When I walk out of the *frutta e verdura,* I'm struck. He said the Sant'Annas were *in season last week.* I had these skinny string beans once. Now they're gone for a year. The cookbook watchword "seasonal" has taken on an immediacy I've never dreamed possible. Ed and I take the baskets up on the terraces and pick dinner. Anselmo has sown waves of lettuces all summer. We can't eat enough; when it bolts, Beppe wields his sickle and bundles the greens for his rabbits. When we cut the chard, *bietole,* it comes back. I like the Italian word for that, *ricrescere;* it sounds as though the stalks are crashing upward through the soil. Fortunately, we planted a lot of cantaloupe and watermelon. Even with gnawing animal raiders, who take one hunk from a melon, we have plenty. As a crop finishes, Anselmo treads down the plants and stalks, letting them decay into the ground.

In spring, we were convinced he was planting too much, and we were right. It's divine. We never have eaten so well. Or as simply. As it turns out, Anselmo's idea of tomatoes is my idea of tomatoes: every day, a heaping basket of perfect red, red tomatoes. I look on these with more pleasure than I had when I saw my new car.

Once upon a time, Italy had no tomatoes. Imagine the poor Etruscans and Romans, the centuries of people who lived before the New World was explored. Their garlic and basil went unpaired with tomatoes!

—FROM *Bella Tuscany*

CONTORNI

BAKED PEPPERS WITH RICOTTA AND BASIL *156*

BAKED TOMATOES AND ARTICHOKES *157*

GARLIC FLAN *158*

GREEN BEANS WITH BLACK OLIVES *159*

SFORMATI *160*

FAVA BEANS WITH POTATOES AND ARTICHOKES *161*

ROASTED VEGETABLES, ESPECIALLY FENNEL *162*

FOUR OTHER ROASTED VEGETABLES *163*

EGGPLANT INVOLTINI *166*

ZUCCHINI WITH LEMON PESTO *168*

SAVORY ROUND ZUCCHINI *169*

FASCICLES OF SUMMER VEGETABLES *170*

DOMENICA'S ROSEMARY POTATOES *171*

CHESTNUTS IN RED WINE *172*

CHARD WITH RAISINS AND ORANGE PEEL *173*

SALAD WITH CHICKPEAS, SUN-DRIED TOMATO, AND GRILLED SHRIMP *174*

FENNEL AND CITRUS SALAD *175*

How lucky that down the Italian peninsula and then into the islands way south, there's a long, long growing season. The selection of gorgeous fruits and vegetables is one of the great delights of cooking here, as I'm sure you know if you've wandered through the weekly markets anywhere in Italy. When I first arrived, I wanted to grab a basket and fill it with the onions like giant pearls, little violet artichokes tender enough to eat raw, fat muscat grapes, wiry wild asparagus, red-speckled borlotti beans, zucchini blossoms like a handful of sunshine, white peaches about to burst with juice, burgundy Treviso lettuce, and pears that look like models for a still-life painting. Even though we now keep a riotously productive *orto* and a small orchard, I still revel in the Thursday market, especially when the artichoke vendors come up from the South in the spring. I buy flats of vegetables to plant, too, and always sample a paper cone of *fritto misto,* crispy fried fish. Like everyone else, I'm compelled to go to market. You just have to be there!

I'm delighted that now, at home in the United States, we have such markets, too. The revival of farmers' markets is the best thing to happen to American food since Julia Child stormed onto the scene with her enthusiasm and can-do attitude. Something about a

farmers' market far transcends the produce on sale, making you feel as though you're participating in an intense community, even if you know no one there. I just sense that I *could* know them, that we're all going to be loving those fresh peas and handfuls of zinnias and mounds of multicolored peppers.

The Tuscan way with vegetables is to let them have their way. With produce from your garden or a farmers' market, that's a good plan. No recipe required. Spinach? Steam it, and add lemon juice and olive oil. *Broccolo romano?* Slice in quarters, steam, toss with chopped anchovies and olive oil. Potatoes? There are no real recipes for potatoes in Tuscany. It's as if the collective voice of all *nonne*, grandmothers, agree: roast or sauté them with olive oil, rosemary, and whole garlic cloves. A little coarse salt. You're done.

Still, with such bounty, many of us have great fun innovating with our eggplants, bushels of potatoes, and tomatoes, tomatoes, tomatoes. *Ripieno*—refill—is what most cooks love to do; eggplant, zucchini, tomatoes, and onions lend themselves to a variety of fillings. *Involtini*—roll-ups—are another favorite. Slice the eggplant or zucchini, lay on prosciutto and mozzarella, roll into a neat wheel, and bake. The local favorite, *sformati*, a kind of a crustless quiche, appears in many guises. Any vegetable will do—carrots look especially appealing. I like making red radicchio and onion *sformati*.

I adore vegetables. There's not a single one I don't like. All the recipes in this Contorni chapter are my personal odes.

GARLIC FLAN

SERVES 6

The whiff of garlic and the silky, creamy texture of this flan accent any robust roasted meats, especially Short Ribs, Tuscan Style (page 129) with Domenica's Rosemary Potatoes (page 171). As a variation, add some sautéed, sliced mushrooms.

1   WHOLE HEAD OF GARLIC
2   CUPS HEAVY CREAM
    A FEW GRATINGS OF NUTMEG
½   TEASPOON SALT
½   TEASPOON PEPPER
4   EGG YOLKS, BEATEN
    EXTRA-VIRGIN OLIVE OIL, FOR THE RAMEKINS

Preheat the oven to 350°F.

Separate the cloves from the head of garlic. Without peeling them, place in boiling water for 7 minutes. Cool, and with your fingers squeeze out the garlic from the skin, crush with a fork, and mince.

Bring the cream and garlic just to a simmer in a medium saucepan. Stir in the nutmeg, salt, and pepper. Remove from the heat, beat a few tablespoons of hot liquid into the egg yolks, then add them to the hot cream. Spoon into six 3½-inch well-oiled ramekins.

Bring 3 cups of water to a boil. Place the ramekins in a 9 x 13-inch baking dish as deep as the ramekins. Pour the boiling water halfway up the sides of the ramekins and bake for 20 to 25 minutes or until set, but soft and silky. Cool for 10 minutes before unmolding, or serve in the ramekins.

GREEN BEANS *with* BLACK OLIVES

SERVES 8

- 2 POUNDS SLENDER GREEN BEANS, TOPPED AND TAILED
- 2 YELLOW ONIONS, FINELY CHOPPED
- 3 TABLESPOONS EXTRA-VIRGIN OLIVE OIL
- 4 TO 5 SLICES PANCETTA

FOR THE MARINADE

- ¾ CUP EXTRA-VIRGIN OLIVE OIL
- ½ TEASPOON SALT
- 1 TEASPOON SUGAR
- ¼ TEASPOON PEPERONCINI (RED PEPPER FLAKES)
- ¼ TEASPOON PEPPER
- 2 TABLESPOONS CHOPPED FRESH TARRAGON LEAVES OR 1 TABLESPOON DRIED
- 2 TABLESPOONS LEMON JUICE
- ½ CUP BLACK OLIVES, PITTED
- JUICE OF 1 ORANGE AND THIN STRIPS OF PEEL

Dragoncello, tarragon, spreads like a brushfire in my herb garden. Although it is not used much in Tuscan cooking, it always has been a favorite of mine. Adjacent to the herb garden, we have a summer plot of green beans and the two hit it off splendidly. I remembered a childhood favorite, my mother's way with marinated green beans, and tweaked it a bit because, at that time in Georgia, we didn't know about extra-virgin olive oil.

Steam the beans just until barely done, about 5 minutes. Empty them into a 9 x 13-inch baking dish. In a small skillet over medium-low heat, sauté the onions in 2 tablespoons of the olive oil for about 3 minutes, or until completely cooked. Mix the onions with the beans in the baking dish.

Combine the marinade ingredients in a jar and shake well. Pour the marinade over the beans and onions, cover, and let rest in the fridge for 6 hours or longer, turning them over several times.

In a small skillet over medium heat, cook the pancetta in the remaining 1 tablespoon olive oil until crisp, about 2 minutes on each side. Drain on absorbent paper towels. Crumble the pancetta over the top and serve chilled or at room temperature.

SFORMATI

The *s* before a consonant at the beginning of an Italian word inserts the negative, as the English *a* does (*atypical*, *asymmetrical*). A *sformato*, then, is not formed; it's out of the mold, unformed. *Sformati* are similar to quiche without the crust. Almost any vegetable can benefit by becoming a *sformato*.

They can be served as a side dish, but we like to turn them out in the middle of an antipasto plate, with a spoonful of tomato sauce on top.

6 EGGS
1 CUP HEAVY CREAM
1 CUP WHOLE MILK
½ CUP *SOFFRITTO* (PAGE 20; ½ RECIPE)
½ CUP (2 OUNCES) GRATED PARMIGIANO-REGGIANO
3 CUPS PREPARED AND SEASONED VEGETABLES:

———

thinly sliced artichoke hearts

zucchini with 1 tablespoon mint and ½ teaspoon lemon zest

red pepper slivers with 5 to 6 torn basil leaves

mushroom slices with 1 tablespoon minced shallot

grated carrot with ½ teaspoon fresh thyme leaves

half a chopped red radicchio and half a minced onion

chopped tomato with 1 tablespoon pesto

———

EXTRA-VIRGIN OLIVE OIL
ALL-PURPOSE FLOUR

Preheat the oven to 350°F. Bring 5 cups of water to a boil.

In a large mixing bowl, lightly beat the eggs. Add the cream, milk, *soffritto*, Parmigiano, and vegetables with their suggested herbs. Stir the mixture well, and spoon it into eight oiled and floured 3½-inch ramekins. Place them in a 10 x 15-inch baking dish as deep as they are. (Or use a muffin tin and make 10 to 12.) Pour about 5 cups of boiling water halfway up the sides of the ramekins. Bake until firm to the touch, about 20 minutes, depending on the vegetable. When slightly cooled, run a thin knife around the edges of the *sformati* and unmold.

FAVA BEANS *with* POTATOES *and* ARTICHOKES

SERVES 6

JUICE OF 1 LEMON, PLUS ADDITIONAL JUICE FOR ACIDULATING WATER

6 SMALL ARTICHOKES, TOP THIRD CUT OFF, TRIMMED OF ALL TOUGH LEAVES, AND QUARTERED

1 POUND SMALL WHITE POTATOES (OR RED NEW POTATOES), PEELED AND QUARTERED

2 POUNDS YOUNG FAVA BEANS, SHELLED

¼ CUP EXTRA-VIRGIN OLIVE OIL

3 SPRING ONIONS OR 2 BUNCHES SCALLIONS, CHOPPED

4 GARLIC CLOVES, MINCED

6 SPRIGS OF THYME

1 TEASPOON SALT

½ TEASPOON PEPPER

Lunch can be a platter of various *salumi*, a bowl of raw unshelled *fave*, a pasta, a round of pecorino, and a glass of wine. At many spring gatherings, the *fave e pecorino* ritual is observed at the end of a light dinner, a simultaneous salad and cheese course. Any time seems to be a good time for this sacred combination.

This recipe could accompany a veal chop or a pork tenderloin, but is a spring vegetable main course, too.

Prepare a bowl of acidulated water. Steam the artichokes until just tender. Drain and set aside in the acidulated water. Steam the potatoes until barely done. Steam the fava beans until almost done.

Heat the olive oil in a large skillet over medium-low heat. Lightly sauté the spring onions or scallions and the garlic 3 to 4 minutes, until translucent. Add the artichokes, potatoes, fava beans, thyme, salt, and pepper. Squeeze the lemon juice over the vegetables. Gently toss the mixture until nicely blended and hot. Turn out into a bowl.

LA FAVA—SPRING FAVORITE

First to arrive—and most loved of the spring vegetables—are the *fave*. The beans are preceded by a lovely flower that in ancient times was thought to bear the letter *theta*, Θ, associated with Thanatos—death. Now we just enjoy the delicate purple and white bloom. In Tuscany, they're called *baccelli* because *fava* is one of the thousands of slang words for "penis." I didn't understand why until we planted them. The beans grow in an erect position instead of dangling.

Once shelled, fresh *fave* don't need to be peeled, although older ones must be blanched and very tediously peeled, bean by bean. Although they still can be good, a bean that must be peeled is basically past its prime and way too much trouble.

ROASTED VEGETABLES,
especially FENNEL

EXTRA-VIRGIN OLIVE OIL
BELL PEPPERS, QUARTERED
SHALLOTS, QUARTERED
FENNEL, QUARTERED
ZUCCHINI AND SUMMER SQUASH, HALVED
EGGPLANT, SLICED
HEADS OF GARLIC, CLEANED OF PAPERY COVERING
TOMATOES, HALVED
FRESH THYME LEAVES
SALT AND PEPPER TO TASTE
LEMON PEEL

The larger the oven, the better to roast a variety of the vegetables of the moment. I've come to prefer oven-roasting to grilling vegetables. The individual flavors are accentuated, while grilling imposes its own smoky taste that can be overwhelming. Oven-roasted fennel is unbelievably good. I find myself stealing a piece as soon as I turn off the oven. Roasting twice as much as you need to serve is a good idea—think of the next day's pasta, salad, and sandwich possibilities.

Preheat the oven to 350°F.

Generously oil a nonstick baking sheet or two with low sides, or line the pan with parchment. Arrange the peppers, shallots, fennel, zucchini and squash, eggplant, garlic, and tomatoes on the sheets. Moisten well with olive oil, and sprinkle with thyme, salt, and pepper. Scatter the lemon peel over the vegetables.

Slide the pan into the oven and roast about 10 minutes, then start testing the squash, zucchini, and tomatoes, removing them to a platter as they are done. Turn the eggplant and peppers. Everything should be done before 30 minutes have passed.

Arrange the vegetables on a platter. Use more olive oil if anything looks needy. The garlic requires hands-on attention. Have your guests pull off the cloves and squeeze them onto bread.

FOUR *other* ROASTED VEGETABLES

ASPARAGUS SPEARS
EXTRA-VIRGIN OLIVE OIL, AS NEEDED
SALT AND PEPPER TO TASTE
GREEN BEANS
ONIONS, ALMOST PEELED
BALSAMIC VINEGAR, AS NEEDED
CAULIFLOWER

Preheat the oven to 400°F for the asparagus and green beans, have it at 350°F for the onions and cauliflower.

Arrange the asparagus spears in a single layer on a parchment-lined baking sheet with low sides. Trickle the olive oil over them and season with salt and pepper. Roast for 5 minutes, or until barely fork-tender, at 400°F.

Steam the green beans until almost done. Shake the steamer until they're dry, season with salt and pepper, and roast on parchment with a dose of olive oil for 5 minutes at 400°F.

Arrange the onions—leave on a layer of the papery skin—in a baking dish. Cut a large *X*-shaped gash in the top of each. Douse liberally with balsamic vinegar and olive oil. Season with salt and pepper. Check the onions while they're roasting, and add more balsamic and oil if they look dry. After 40 minutes at 350°F, a fork should pierce through with little resistance.

Cut off the bottom of the cauliflower and then cut it into florets. Place them on oiled parchment in a low-sided baking pan. Season with olive oil, salt, and pepper and cover the pan with aluminum foil. Bake for 15 minutes covered at 350°F, then remove the foil, turn the cauliflower over, and bake another 10 minutes, or until tender with crispy edges.

Since my friend Susan Wyler, author of several cookbooks, taught me to roast asparagus in the oven, I've rarely steamed it. Even burned and crisp, they're delicious. Little green beans also benefit from a run in the oven. With about two hundred onions growing like mad in the garden, I've taken to roasting them frequently; the contrasting flavor of balsamic vinegar adds a sweet surprise. Surround a roast chicken with a ring of these onions. Unlike in the previous recipe, these vegetables roast separately.

EGGPLANT INVOLTINI

SERVES 8

Italians love the *involtini* concept—something filled and rolled. I experimented with this idea, since I had a nice firm and gigantic eggplant. For this dish, choose the brick-shaped part-skim mozzarella because it has less moisture. For beauty, tie the *involtini* with chives.

- 3 TABLESPOONS EXTRA-VIRGIN OLIVE OIL, PLUS MORE FOR THE PARCHMENT
- 1 LARGE EGGPLANT, CUT LENGTHWISE INTO 8 SLICES
- 1 TABLESPOON FRESH OREGANO LEAVES OR 1½ TEASPOONS DRIED
- 1 TEASPOON SALT
- ½ TEASPOON PEPPER
- 8 TOMATOES OR 1 28-OUNCE CAN WHOLE TOMATOES ALMOST DRAINED OF LIQUID, CHOPPED
- 1 YELLOW ONION, CHOPPED
- 1 GARLIC CLOVE, MINCED
- 8 SLICES PROSCIUTTO
- 8 SLICES PART-SKIM MOZZARELLA FRESH CHIVES
- ¼ CUP (1 OUNCE) GRATED PARMIGIANO-REGGIANO

Preheat the oven to 400°F. Oil a parchment-lined baking sheet.

Place the eggplant slices on the pan and brush on both sides with 2 tablespoons of the olive oil. Sprinkle on the oregano, salt, and pepper. Bake for 10 minutes, turning once. They will then be supple.

While the eggplant is in the oven, make a simple tomato sauce by whirring the tomatoes briefly in a food processor. In a medium skillet over medium heat, sauté the onion for 2 to 3 minutes in the remaining 1 tablespoon of olive oil, then add the garlic and sauté for another minute. Stir in the tomatoes and cook the mixture briefly, just to blend flavors, about 2 minutes.

Remove the eggplant from the oven. Lower the oven temperature to 350°F.

On each eggplant piece, place a slice of prosciutto and a slice of mozzarella. Roll the pieces from the small end forward, and secure the neat little bundle with a toothpick or by tying a chive around it.

Slather the bottom of a 9 x 13-inch baking dish with some of the tomato sauce, and arrange the *involtini* seam side down. Over each bundle spread some more tomato sauce and a scattering of the Parmigiano. Warm well in the oven, about 15 minutes. *Finito!*

ZUCCHINI *with* LEMON PESTO

SERVES 8

Who could complain that zucchini is too prolific? When you grow it, you have the pleasure of picking the zucchini when they are firm and small. Then you can slice them into nickel- or quarter-size coins and warm them through in extra-virgin olive oil— the simplest preparation for this most compliant vegetable, especially with a generous sprinkling of one of its favorite companions, mint.

8 TO 10   SLENDER ZUCCHINI, GRATED OR FINELY SLICED
3 TO 4   SPRING ONIONS, MINCED

FOR THE LEMON PESTO

JUICE AND ZEST OF 2 LEMONS
1   HANDFUL OF BASIL LEAVES, TORN
5 TO 6   GARLIC CLOVES
¼   CUP HAZELNUTS, TOASTED
3   TABLESPOONS EXTRA-VIRGIN OLIVE OIL
SALT AND PEPPER TO TASTE
¼   CUP (1 OUNCE) GRATED PARMIGIANO-REGGIANO

If the zucchini are grated, squeeze out some of the liquid. Steam the zucchini and onions in a steamer basket until they are just done, about 4 minutes.

Make the lemon pesto. In a mortar or food processor, combine the lemon juice and zest, basil, garlic, hazelnuts, olive oil, salt, and pepper and blend well, until the consistency of regular pesto. Work in the cheese only at the end. Combine the pesto with the vegetables in a large skillet and heat through on medium low, about 5 minutes. Serve warm or at room temperature.

SAVORY ROUND ZUCCHINI

  6 ROUND ZUCCHINI
     JUICE OF 1 LEMON
 ¼ CUP EXTRA-VIRGIN OLIVE OIL
 ½ TEASPOON SALT
 ½ TEASPOON PEPPER
  1 CUP *BESCIAMELLA* (PAGE 24)
 ¼ POUND SLICED HAM, IN SLIVERS
  1 CARROT, MINCED
 ¼ CUP FRESH OR FROZEN PEAS
  4 OUNCES FONTINA, CUBED
  2 TABLESPOONS MINCED FLAT-LEAF PARSLEY
 ¼ CUP (1 OUNCE) GRATED PARMIGIANO-REGGIANO
  3 TABLESPOONS BREADCRUMBS, TOASTED

Preheat the oven to 350°F. Bring a medium saucepan of water to a boil.

Line a 9 x 13-inch baking dish with parchment. Slice off the stem-end tops of the zucchini and save them. With a teaspoon, hollow out and discard the interiors.

Boil the zucchini for 3 minutes. They should be slightly cooked but still firm. Remove and drain the zucchini. Pour the lemon juice and a little olive oil into the hollows. Season with the salt and pepper.

To the *besciamella* in a large mixing bowl, add the ham, carrot, peas, fontina, parsley, and Parmigiano. Mix well. Fill the zucchini with the vegetable mixture, and top with the bread-crumbs. Place the zucchini shells in the baking dish. Drizzle them with the rest of the olive oil, and place their little hats on top. Bake for 30 minutes or until the zucchini are cooked.

Round zucchini keep their firmness better than long ones. Filled with vegetables, these pretties make a happy addition to a platter of grilled meat or they can stand alone as a light first course. As an alternative to this ham and fontina recipe, simply fill the prepared rounds with sautéed onion, crunchy bread-crumbs, parsley, Parmigiano, and chopped tomatoes, drizzle with olive oil, and bake as described.

FASCICLES *of* SUMMER VEGETABLES

MAKES 10 BUNDLES

A bundle of iron sticks (*fasces* in Latin) with a protruding ax head was discovered in a seventh-century B.C. Etruscan tomb, the earliest known image of the fascicle. The Romans adopted the symbol as a sign of authority, power, and unity.

Later, the image gave its name to the Fascist Party. It appears on war monuments all over Italy, but you can see it in unlikely places: two fascicles adorn the seal of the U.S. Senate. It is on the old mercury dime, and also on the Lincoln Memorial.

Right now, let's think instead of the little bundles of handwritten poems that Emily Dickinson rolled into fascicles, tied with string, and hid in her drawer. And of these chive-tied summer vegetables, so delicious that Etruscans, Fascists, Lincoln, and Emily Dickinson would have relished a big helping.

1	LARGE YELLOW BELL PEPPER
1	LARGE RED BELL PEPPER
4	CARROTS
4	YOUNG ZUCCHINI
½	POUND SLENDER GREEN BEANS, TOPPED AND TAILED
10	LONG CHIVE STEMS, PLUS SNIPPED CHIVES FOR GARNISH
¼	CUP EXTRA-VIRGIN OLIVE OIL
	JUICE OF 1 LEMON
½	TEASPOON SALT
	SEVERAL SPRIGS OF THYME

Cut the peppers, carrots, and zucchini into the same size and thickness as the green beans. Stack in separate piles in a large steamer and lightly steam the peppers and carrots for 8 minutes, adding the zucchini only for the last 2 to 3 minutes. Make sure the vegetables stay taut and crisp.

When cool enough to touch, bundle several of each vegetable, and then tie with a chive stem.

In a jar, shake together the olive oil, lemon juice, and salt. Arrange the fascicles on a platter and pour the dressing over them. Sprinkle the snipped chives and thyme sprigs on top. Serve warm or at room temperature.

Domenica's ROSEMARY POTATOES

SERVES 6

- ½ CUP EXTRA-VIRGIN OLIVE OIL
- 6 RUSSET OR YUKON GOLD POTATOES, PEELED AND CUT INTO LARGE DICE
- ½ TEASPOON PEPPER
- 2 TABLESPOONS MINCED FRESH ROSEMARY OR 1 TABLESPOON DRIED
  SEA SALT TO TASTE

Heat the olive oil in a 12-inch skillet over medium heat until hot but not smoking. Cook the potatoes, standing by with a spatula to turn them occasionally so that they don't stick as they brown. As they begin to crisp, after about 10 minutes, season with the pepper and rosemary. Continue to toss around, testing for doneness, usually 20 to 25 more minutes. Add the sea salt before serving.

Domenica uses a cast-iron pan for her crisp potatoes, which are a cross between fried and sautéed. The usual Tuscan way with potatoes is oven-roasted. Mix large-diced potatoes with a couple of table-spoons of olive oil, fresh rosemary, salt, and pepper. On a parchment-lined baking sheet, roast them at 375°F for 20 to 30 minutes, turning once or twice. Tried—and truly excellent. But somehow, the black iron works another kind of magic. I've come to prefer Domenica's way.

CHESTNUTS *in* RED WINE

SERVES 8

30 to 40   FRESH CHESTNUTS OR A 14-OUNCE JAR
          OF CHESTNUTS
½   BOTTLE RED WINE (OR TO COVER)

We gather baskets of chestnuts in the fall and we have to hurry—we've got competition from every wild boar in the area.

Even though I live near a chestnut forest, they still seem luxurious. Our first year here, we bought a chestnut pan for the fireplace and roasted a few every night in winter. Scoring the shell before they're put in the pan ensures they'll peel easily when roasted. Many cookbooks advise roasting chestnuts for up to an hour! But they're ready quickly—15 minutes or so, depending on their size and how hot the coals are. Roasted chestnuts call for a meditative glass of a Nicolis Ambrosan, Amarone or Casanova di Neri, Brunello di Montalcino Tenuta Nuova.

Coddled in red wine, chestnuts taste like the essence of autumn. Arrange them around a pork loin or a roasted chicken, or include them in your turkey's stuffing.

Before roasting, chestnuts must have their skin sliced; otherwise they'll explode. With a short-bladed knife, cut a slit or *X* on the flat side.

Pile them in a chestnut roaster or in a perforated pan, the kind used for vegetables on the outdoor grill. Roast them over hot coals (not an open flame) for about 7 minutes, occasionally shaking the pan well to redistribute the chestnuts. After another 5 minutes, pierce one with a knife. It should go in quite easily. (Alternatively, use the oven, preheated to 450°F. Spread the scored chestnuts in a pan. Check at 20 minutes and then check every 5 minutes.)

Pour the roasted chestnuts into a bowl, let them cool only long enough to handle, then peel.

In a medium saucepan, simmer the chestnuts, partially covered, in just enough red wine to submerge them for 15 minutes—long enough for the flavors to intertwine. Pour off most of the wine.

CHARD *with* RAISINS *and* ORANGE PEEL

SERVES 4

- ½ CUP RAISINS
- 2 TABLESPOONS *VIN SANTO* OR ORANGE JUICE
- 2 LARGE BUNCHES CHARD
- 2 TABLESPOONS EXTRA-VIRGIN OLIVE OIL
- 1 YELLOW ONION, DICED
- ½ TEASPOON SALT
- ½ TEASPOON PEPPER
  PEEL OF 1 ORANGE
- ¼ CUP PINE NUTS, TOASTED

Soak the raisins for 15 minutes in the 2 tablespoons *vin santo* or orange juice.

Cut off the tough ends of the chard stems, and then slice the rest into 1-inch pieces. Steam the chard until the leaves are limp, about 7 minutes. Cool, squeeze out the excess water, then coarsely chop the chard and set it aside.

In a large skillet over medium heat (while the chard is steaming), cook the stems in the olive oil with the onion for 5 minutes, or until the stems are al dente. Add them to the cooked chard leaves and season with salt and pepper. Mix in the peel, raisins, *vin santo*, and pine nuts. Cook, covered, on medium-low heat, for 2 to 3 minutes to heat through.

Chard grows easily. How gratifying that it's cut-and-come-again. If you have a plot for chard, you learn to harvest a huge quantity and steam an enormous potful at once. Then you drain and cool the much-reduced clump of greens, squeeze out the water, and form softball-size balls. What a boon for the cook. You can freeze these balls individually in plastic wrap. They're then ready for soups or this very typical sauté. Always use most of the stems, cut into small hunks. Kale works just as well in this recipe.

SALAD *with* CHICKPEAS, SUN-DRIED TOMATO, *and* GRILLED SHRIMP

When I take the first bite of this salad, I feel that I'm sitting under the great old Mediterranean sun, tasting the sea and the land at once. Texture is everything in a salad; this one delivers several: crunchy chickpeas, crisp greens, vibrant slivers of sun-dried tomato, and tender shrimp.

1	POUND MEDIUM SHRIMP, PEELED AND CLEANED
6	TABLESPOONS EXTRA-VIRGIN OLIVE OIL
¾	TEASPOON SALT
¾	TEASPOON PEPPER
1	BAY LEAF
1	TEASPOON FRESH OREGANO LEAVES OR ½ TEASPOON DRIED
1	TABLESPOON BALSAMIC VINEGAR
4	SPRING ONIONS, FINELY CHOPPED
1½	CUPS CHICKPEAS, COOKED AND SEASONED (SEE PAGE 24)
¼	CUP SUN-DRIED TOMATOES, THINLY SLICED AND RECONSTITUTED IN ¼ CUP OLIVE OIL
10	OUNCES MIXED CRISP AND PUNGENT GREENS, SUCH AS ROMAINE, ARUGULA, LITTLE GEM, BUTTER, MÂCHE, AND FRISÉE
	PEEL OF 1 LEMON, CUT INTO STRIPS FOR GARNISH

In a large skillet over medium heat, cook the shrimp in 2 tablespoons of the olive oil with ½ teaspoon salt, ½ teaspoon pepper, the bay leaf, and oregano, stirring occasionally for about 5 minutes, or until the shrimp turn pink.

In a small bowl, whisk together the remaining 4 tablespoons olive oil, the balsamic vinegar, spring onions, and remaining ¼ teaspoon salt and ¼ teaspoon pepper.

In the same skillet, mix the chickpeas, tomatoes, and shrimp with half of the salad dressing. Toss the greens with the other half of the dressing and arrange on six plates. Spoon the shrimp mixture on top and garnish with strips of lemon peel.

FENNEL *and* CITRUS SALAD

SERVES 8

2 TO 3 FENNEL BULBS, THINLY SLICED, FRONDS RESERVED
FOR GARNISH

1 BLOOD ORANGE, PEELED, SLICED, AND SEEDED

2 TANGERINES, PEELED, SLICED, AND SEEDED

1 SHALLOT, MINCED

ZEST OF 1 LEMON

ZEST OF 1 ORANGE

1 TEASPOON FRESH THYME LEAVES OR
½ TEASPOON DRIED

FOR THE DRESSING

4 TABLESPOONS EXTRA-VIRGIN OLIVE OIL

2 TABLESPOONS CHAMPAGNE VINEGAR

JUICE OF 1 SMALL TANGERINE

SALT AND PEPPER TO TASTE

JUICE OF 1 LEMON

The anise taste of fennel plays so well with the tropical citrus flavors and the slight bite of shallot. Use any other orange, if a blood orange is unavailable.

Put the fennel in a large bowl with the sliced oranges and tangerines. Stir in the shallot, zests, and thyme. In a small bowl, whisk the dressing ingredients. Pour it over the fennel and orange mixture, and gently toss. Arrange the salad in a shallow serving bowl and garnish with fennel fronds.

DOLCI

The long stretch of summer lunches calls for a long *tavola*, the longer the better, because inevitably guests gather—friends from home, a relative's friends from somewhere who thought they'd say hello since they were in the area, and new friends, sometimes with friends of *theirs.* Add another handful of pasta to the boiling pot, add a plate, a tumbler, find another chair. The table and the kitchen can oblige.

I have considered my table, its ideals, as well as its dimensions. If I were a child, I would want to lift up the tablecloth and crawl under the unending table, into the flaxen light where I could crouch and listen to the loud laughs, clinks, and grown-up talk, hear over and over "*Salute*" and "*Cin-cin*" traveling around the chairs, stare at knee-caps and walking shoes and flowered skirts hiked up to catch a breeze. Such a table should accommodate the wanderings of a large dog. At the end, you need room for an enormous vase of all the flowers in bloom. The width should allow platters to meander from hand to hand, stopping where they will, and numerous water and wine bottles to accumulate over the hours. You need room for a bowl of cool water to dip the grapes and pears into, and a little covered dish to keep the bugs off the Gorgonzola. No one cares if olive pits are flung into the distance. The best wardrobe for such a table runs to pale linens or blue checks, not dead white that takes in too much glare. If the table is long enough, everything can be brought out at once, and no one has to run back and forth. Then the table is set for primary pleasure: lingering meals, under the trees at noon. The open air confers an ease, a relaxation and freedom. You're your own guest, the way summer ought to be.

—FROM *Under the Tuscan Sun*

DOLCI

LEMON HAZELNUT GELATO *182*

PEACH GELATO *183*

BASIL AND MINT SORBETTO *184*

CLEMENTINE SORBETTO *185*

STRAWBERRY SEMIFREDDO *186*

PANNA COTTA *187*

WINTER PEARS IN VINO NOBILE *188*

TULIP SHELLS WITH THREE BERRIES *189*

PEACHES WITH ALMOND CREAM *190*

SACRED PEACHES *190*

RUSTIC APPLE BREAD PUDDING *191*

TWO CRUSTS FOR TARTS *192*

    PASTA FROLLA *192*

    FLAKY PASTRY *194*

FOLDED FRUIT TART WITH MASCARPONE *195*

SILVIA'S RICOTTA TART *196*

TORTA DELLA NONNA *197*

IVAN'S BIG BLACKBERRY CROSTATA *198*

APPLE IN A CAGE *199*

RASPBERRY ALMOND ROULADE *200*

FIG AND WALNUT TART *201*

MASSIMO AND DANIELA'S WINE CAKE *204*

ED'S CANTUCCI *206*

IL FALCONIERE'S CHOCOLATE CAKE WITH VANILLA SAUCE *207*

CHERRIES STEEPED IN RED WINE *209*

LEMON CAKE *210*

After dinner in summer, someone will divide a watermelon into wedges. In winter, out comes a bowl of tangerines and a chunk of pecorino. Fruits of all seasons—cherries, grapes, plums, figs, pears, persimmons—are thought by Tuscans to bring a *cena* to a proper close. Not that they don't like desserts. They tend to enjoy them for an occasional afternoon indulgence or when guests are at the table. The classics are *panna cotta* (cooked cream), *crostata* (jam tart), *torta della nonna* (custard in a pine-nut–studded crust), and gelato. When our Italian friends eat gelato, it's usually after a movie or concert in the piazza.

Because of the tendency away from sweets, it took me years to appreciate the astonishing range of local *dolci*. Dinner by dinner, holiday by holiday, our friends served forth an ever-changing array of desserts. Chefs brought out their favorites. Some desserts are made for particular occasions. Serpent-shaped pastries filled with almond paste (oh, heavy!) are always on the table after Christmas dinner. Everyone has a bite. Before Lent, and only then, *cenci,* crunchy fried pastry bows, appear. In Cortona, most everyone serving a Sunday family lunch visits Pasticceria Banchelli for their famous cream-filled meringues. I've not included this recipe because I've never been able to replicate their airy confection. Maybe it's the eggs, maybe it's the North Carolina humidity, or maybe it's Gianni's ability to whisk like an angel. If you ever go to Cortona, try them.

The recipes in Dolci accumulated slowly, as Giusi introduced us to her berry-filled pastry tulips, as Silvia served us her ricotta tart and her steamed chocolate cake.

We must have had a hundred *crostate* at La Casita, the Cardinalis' house. Donatella makes the best *cantucci.* The wine cake comes from Daniela and Massimo's Bar Tuscher on the main street of Cortona. Maybe because she was born near Naples, with its Bourbon inheritance, Gilda prefers more elaborate roulades with cream and berries or large tarts overlapped with strawberries, kiwis, bananas, and raspberries.

Many desserts we improvised from a plethora of fruit—cherries steeped in red wine, peaches filled with almond cream, and winter pears in red wine. Some come from travels: we tasted Apple in a Cage in the Veneto, semifreddo in Naples. The one that traveled the farthest is the Lemon Cake, all the way from my mother's kitchen in Georgia. She used to say, as she served one of her Deep South wonders, "Sweets to the sweet."

I used to think dessert had to be chocolate. That's still hard to top, but I've come to love the simplicity of fruit on its own—a slice of pineapple with a drop or so of fine bal-

samic vinegar, or a handful of cherries served with a bowl of water for rinsing, figs, and a dab of Gorgonzola. Still, a celebration calls for something, well—celebratory, and Tuscans flat-out know how to celebrate with a soulful and stupendous finale.

LEMON HAZELNUT GELATO

SERVES 8 TO 10 (ABOUT 2 QUARTS)

Super rich, this gelato makes me want to give up my citizenship and decamp permanently. Even people who claim not to like ice cream slip into a swoon over this one.

As in the Clementine Sorbetto (page 185), I like to intensify the fruit's taste by adding a little liqueur of the same fruit. When you toast the hazelnuts, watch them carefully; they burn easily. After five minutes, wrap them in a dishtowel and rub off the fine brown skins.

- **6** EGG YOLKS
- **1½** CUPS SUGAR
- **1** QUART HALF-AND-HALF
- **1** TABLESPOON FRANGELICO (HAZELNUT LIQUEUR) OR 1 TEASPOON VANILLA EXTRACT
- **2** CUPS HEAVY CREAM
- **1½** CUPS HAZELNUTS, TOASTED AND CHOPPED
- ZEST OF 1 LEMON

In a medium bowl, beat the yolks and sugar until nicely incorporated. In a large saucepan, bring the half-and-half almost to a boil over medium-high heat. Quickly remove from the heat. Whisk ½ cup of the heated cream into the eggs and sugar, and then stir it all back into the hot half-and-half. Lower the heat to a good simmer, and stir the mixture until it thickens and coats a wooden spoon, about 5 minutes. Don't allow it to boil. Set aside and whisk in the Frangelico or vanilla and the heavy cream and then the hazelnuts and lemon zest.

Chill the mixture thoroughly (7 to 8 hours). Stir well again and process as your ice cream machine requires.

PEACH GELATO

SERVES 14 (ABOUT 3 QUARTS)

- 3 EGGS, BEATEN
- 1 CUP SUGAR
- 1 QUART WHOLE MILK
- 1 CUP HEAVY CREAM
- 1 TABLESPOON ALL-PURPOSE FLOUR
- 1/8 TEASPOON SALT
- 2 QUARTS PEELED AND PITTED PEACHES
   JUICE OF 1 LEMON
- 1 TEASPOON VANILLA EXTRACT

*I*s *anything* better than homemade peach ice cream? You can use other fruits, but why? Just be sure to use ripe peaches, white if possible.

Beat together the eggs and half of the sugar in a small bowl. In a large saucepan, bring the milk and cream almost to a boil over medium-high heat. Quickly remove from the heat. Whisk ½ cup of the heated milk/cream into the egg and sugar mixture, then stir it all back into the saucepan. Stir in the flour, salt, and ¼ cup of sugar. Lower the heat to a good simmer, and stir the mixture until it thickens and coats a wooden spoon, about 10 minutes. Don't allow it to boil. Set aside.

Purée the peaches with the lemon juice, the remaining ¼ cup of sugar, and the vanilla. Fold and blend the fruit into the custard mixture. Chill the mixture thoroughly (7 to 8 hours). Stir well again and process as your ice cream machine requires.

BASIL *and* MINT SORBETTO

SERVES 8 (ABOUT 1½ PINTS)

3 CUPS WATER
1 CUP SUGAR
½ CUP MINT LEAVES, PLUS ADDITIONAL LEAVES FOR GARNISH
½ CUP BASIL LEAVES
1 TABLESPOON LEMON JUICE

I tasted this unlikely but tantalizing sorbetto at the ancient *fattoria*-turned-restaurant Locanda dell'Amorosa, in nearby Sinalunga. At a wedding dinner, it was served after the pasta and fish courses and before the *secondo*. The next day I tried to duplicate it at home. More informally, at our house, it's an icy palate cleanser after the pasta on a warm summer night.

In a medium saucepan, make a sugar syrup by boiling together 1 cup of water with the sugar. Simmer for about 5 minutes, stirring constantly, until the sugar dissolves. Put the saucepan in the refrigerator to cool.

Purée the ½ cup of mint and ½ cup of basil leaves in 1 cup of water, and then add the remaining cup of water and the lemon juice. Purée another 3 to 4 seconds to blend well. Pour this into the saucepan with the sugar syrup, and chill well for 5 to 6 hours. Stir well again and process as your ice cream machine requires. Scoop into martini glasses or any small glass dishes and garnish with mint leaves. Serve immediately.

CLEMENTINE SORBETTO

In the winter, when clementines roll in from Sicily, I like to serve this easy sorbetto.

If I'd grown up in Tuscany, I'm sure the fragrance of citrus would be indelibly associated with Christmas. The holiday decorations on all the shops in Assisi are lemon boughs. Against the pale stones, the fruit glows like lighted ornaments and the scent of lemons infuses the cold air. In Cortona, baskets of clementines brighten the streets. Bars are squeezing that most opulent of juices, the dark blood orange.

This ethereal sorbetto, which works wonders as a pause in a winter dinner or as a dessert, also can be made with blood orange or other juices. Try to find untreated clementines; in the United States, the peel is often coated with a chemical-based wax.

SERVES 6 (MAKES 3½ CUPS)

- 2 CUPS COLD WATER
- 1 CUP SUGAR
- 2 CUPS CLEMENTINE OR TANGERINE JUICE, PLUS ZEST OF 3 CLEMENTINES
- 2 TABLESPOONS LEMON JUICE, PLUS ZEST SPRIGS OF MINT OR THYME, FOR GARNISH

In a medium saucepan, make a sugar syrup by boiling together 1 cup of water with the sugar. Simmer for about 5 minutes, stirring constantly until the sugar dissolves. Add the other 1 cup of water and mix in the citrus juices and zests. Chill for 5 to 6 hours. Stir well again and process as your ice cream machine requires. Scoop the sorbetto into martini glasses or any small glass dishes and garnish with mint or thyme sprigs.

STRAWBERRY SEMIFREDDO

SERVES 8

Not gelato, not sorbetto—semi-freddo occupies a niche. The light and creamy texture melts fast in your mouth, leaving the essential freshness of the fruit. It's easy, too, since you need no ice cream machine. Semi-freddo keeps well in the freezer for a week.

1½ PINTS STRAWBERRIES, HULLED
1 TABLESPOON ORANGE JUICE
1¼ CUPS SUGAR
4 EGGS
¼ CUP WHOLE MILK
1 TEASPOON VANILLA EXTRACT
½ CUP (4 OUNCES) MASCARPONE
1½ CUPS HEAVY CREAM

Purée the strawberries (reserving and refrigerating several pretty ones) with the orange juice and 2 tablespoons of the sugar. Chill the purée in a large bowl until ready to use.

Bring water almost to a boil in the bottom of a double boiler, then

lower the heat to a good simmer. In the top, beat the eggs with the remaining sugar, the milk, and vanilla. Whisk continuously for 10 to 14 minutes, or until the mixture thickens and forms trailing ribbons. Reserve ¼ cup of the strawberry purée, then whisk the egg mixture into the purée. Cool the mixture in the fridge about 1½ hours.

Line a 9 x 5-inch loaf pan with plastic wrap, leaving a few inches overhanging the sides.

When the strawberry-egg mixture has cooled, whisk in the mascarpone. In a separate bowl, whip the cream until firm peaks form. Fold the cream into the strawberry and mascar-pone mixture.

Pour the semifreddo into the pan, and freeze for at least 4 hours. Unmold by loosening the plastic wrap, then inverting the pan onto a serving dish. Add the reserved strawberries to the remaining ¼ cup strawberry purée and spoon this over the semifreddo in the dish or over individual servings.

PANNA COTTA

SERVES 6

	UNSALTED BUTTER, FOR THE RAMEKINS
3¼	CUPS HEAVY CREAM
	ZEST OF 1 LEMON OR ORANGE
	PINCH OF SALT
½	CUP PLUS 1 TABLESPOON SUGAR
2	TEASPOONS VANILLA EXTRACT
2½	TEASPOONS UNFLAVORED GELATIN
3	TABLESPOONS TEPID WHOLE MILK
1	CUP RASPBERRIES

Cooked cream is similar to crème brûlée, without the crunch of the caramelized sugar. *Panna cotta* more than compensates with its velvety texture. This is a classic Tuscan dessert. Serve it with a dollop of puréed and sweetened berries, or simply with a few whole berries scattered on top.

I wonder if *panna cotta*'s popularity is due partly to its under-ten-minute prep time.

Butter six 3½-inch ramekins.

In a medium saucepan over medium heat, bring the cream, zest, salt, and ½ cup sugar almost to a boil. The cream will be bubbling slightly around the edges. Reduce the heat to medium low, and stir the mixture for 5 minutes, until the cream is tinted with the zest. Stir in the vanilla and remove the saucepan from the heat.

In a small dish, dissolve the gelatin in the milk for a minute and then add to it a couple of spoonfuls of the hot cream. Whisk with a fork, and then add the gelatin mixture to the saucepan. Continue to stir until all the gelatin is dissolved. Divide the cream among the ramekins. Cool on the counter or in the fridge until set.

Serve the *panna cotta* in the ramekins or unmold by loosening the sides with a thin knife. If you're serving them later, cover the ramekins with plastic wrap and keep them in the fridge. When serving, sprinkle the remaining tablespoon of sugar over the raspberries and decorate the top of each *panna cotta* with the berries.

WINTER PEARS *in* VINO NOBILE

SERVES 6

Poached pears look sensuous, and tinted with red wine, downright sexy. In winter, their taste is heightened when served along with some Gorgonzola, toasted bread, and walnuts roasted with olive oil and salt. In summer, serve the pears with sweetened mascarpone (page 209) and curls of lemon peel.

6 FIRM PEARS, PEELED, WITH STEMS LEFT ON
¼ CUP LEMON JUICE, PLUS THIN STRIPS OF LEMON PEEL, FOR GARNISH
1 CUP RED WINE
¼ CUP SUGAR
¼ CUP CURRANTS, EITHER RED OR BLACK
1 VANILLA BEAN, SPLIT IN HALF LENGTHWISE
3 OR 4 CLOVES

Cut a small slice off the bottoms of the pears, so they can stand upright. In a large saucepan off the heat, arrange the pears, and pour the lemon juice and then the wine over them. Sprinkle on the sugar. Add the currants, vanilla bean, and cloves to the wine. Turn the heat to medium to bring the wine to a simmer.

Cover the saucepan and maintain the simmer for 15 minutes (or longer, depending on the size and ripeness of the pears). Midway, turn the pears on their sides and baste several times with the wine. When they are rosy and still slightly firm, transfer them to serving dishes. Discard the cloves and vanilla bean. Pour some wine syrup and currants over each pear, and garnish with thin strips of lemon peel.

TULIP SHELLS *with* THREE BERRIES

SERVES 8

FOR THE TULIP SHELLS

- 1 CUP (2 STICKS) UNSALTED BUTTER
- 1¾ CUPS CONFECTIONERS' SUGAR
- 4 EGG WHITES
- 1¾ CUPS ALL-PURPOSE FLOUR

FOR THE FILLING

- 4 CUPS MIXED BLACKBERRIES, RASPBERRIES, AND STRAWBERRIES
- 4 TABLESPOONS SUPERFINE OR LIGHT BROWN SUGAR
- ¾ CUP HEAVY CREAM, WHIPPED
- 5 TABLESPOONS GRANULATED SUGAR
- ¾ CUP (6 OUNCES) MASCARPONE
  STRIPS OF LEMON OR ORANGE PEEL, FOR GARNISH

Ed watched Giusi make these tulip-shaped cookie shells, *tulipani,* for a party. She filled them with strawberries and cream. The next day he surprised me by making them himself—his first venture into pastry. Peaches, pears, or raspberries work just as well. Maybe there is a prettier dessert, but I don't know of one.

With any leftover batter, bake crisp, silver-dollar–size cookies, adding a few sliced almonds to each.

Preheat the oven to 350°F.

Make the tulip shells. Melt the butter in a medium saucepan. Remove from the heat, and stir in the confectioners' sugar. Whisk in the egg whites. Add the flour and beat until the batter forms ribbons, about 2 minutes. On a large baking sheet, butter four 7-inch circles. Spoon ¼ cup of the batter onto each circle, and with the back of the spoon, spread it evenly, covering the circle. It will look like a crêpe. Bake for 10 minutes, until slightly browned around the edges and pale gold in the middle.

Gingerly lift off a circle with a spatula. Immediately place it on a dishtowel that you're holding in your hand. With care, place the bottom of a 3-inch-diameter glass into the center of the circle, gently pressing down your fingers to mold the tulip. After 30 seconds, the tulip will harden enough to handle. Repeat with the rest of the circles, setting them aside to cool. Allow the pan to cool before baking your second batch, or use a different sheet. Repeat the process to make the remaining 4 *tulipani.* When all the *tulipani* are completely cool, put them on a platter and cover with plastic wrap, otherwise they will become soft. (They will keep for two days this way.)

Make the filling. In a small bowl, mix the berries with the superfine or brown sugar. In a separate bowl, whip the cream until soft peaks form, sweetening it as you whisk with 2 tablespoons of the granulated sugar. With a wooden spoon, beat in the mascarpone with the remaining granulated sugar. Spoon about 2 heaping tablespoons into each tulip and top with the fruit. Garnish with a dollop of the mascarpone and the citrus peel.

PEACHES *with* ALMOND CREAM

SERVES 6

This looks like what the angels eat, and the taste is unctuous and luxurious.

Those angels might also pour some liquid orange blossoms—Conte Emo Capodilista, Donna Daria Fior d'Arancio Passito.

FOR THE FILLING

- 1 CUP (8 OUNCES) MASCARPONE
- JUICE OF ½ LEMON
- ¼ CUP HEAVY CREAM
- ¼ CUP SUPERFINE SUGAR
- ½ CUP SLICED ALMONDS, TOASTED AND COOLED
- 1½ CUPS CRUSHED ALMOND COOKIES, SUCH AS AMARETTI

- 1 CUP WHITE WINE OR PROSECCO
- 2 TABLESPOONS SUGAR
- 6 LARGE PEACHES, PREFERABLY WHITE, RIPE BUT FIRM, PEELED, HALVED, AND PITTED
- MINT LEAVES, FOR GARNISH

In a bowl, mix all the filling ingredients and chill for 30 minutes.

Bring the wine and sugar to a boil in a 12-inch skillet, and then lower the heat to a simmer. Add the peaches and poach them for 3 to 4 minutes, frequently spooning liquid over them. Remove peaches from the liquid and let them cool, reserving the liquid.

Spoon mascarpone mixture into the centers of 6 of the peach halves, and then cover with the other halves. Spoon poaching liquid over each. Garnish with mint.

SACRED PEACHES

SERVES 8

No wine cupboard in Tuscany lacks a bottle of *vin santo*, sacred wine. One of Italy's best is made at Avignonesi, just outside Cortona. Traditionally sipped with *cantucci, vin santo* also adds to desserts a nutty depth of flavor, as in this instant summery treat.

- 8 RIPE, FIRM PEACHES, PEELED, PITTED, AND QUARTERED
- JUICE OF 1 LEMON
- A FEW GRATINGS OF NUTMEG
- ½ CUP *VIN SANTO*
- 1 CUP SUPERFINE SUGAR
- 2 PINTS ALMOND, HAZELNUT, OR VANILLA ICE CREAM, SLIGHTLY SOFTENED

In a medium bowl, toss the peaches with the lemon juice, nutmeg, and *vin santo.* Melt the sugar in a large cast-iron pan over low heat, stirring it until it turns tawny. Add the peaches. Raise the heat to medium low, and stirring gently, cook the peaches for about 5 minutes, until slightly softened. Cool the inebriated fruit until ready to serve.

In glass dessert bowls, layer the ice cream and peaches.

RUSTIC APPLE
BREAD PUDDING

   5 CRISP BAKING APPLES
      JUICE OF 2 LEMONS
      A FEW GRATINGS OF NUTMEG
   ¾ CUP SUGAR
  12 TABLESPOONS (1½ STICKS) UNSALTED BUTTER,
      PLUS ADDITIONAL FOR THE PAN
   1 CUP WALNUTS, TOASTED AND COARSELY CHOPPED
   ¼ CUP APPLE CIDER OR WATER
   1 LOAF LEFTOVER BREAD, ANY HARD CRUSTS REMOVED,
      CUT INTO 1½-INCH CUBES
   4 EGGS
  1¼ CUPS WHOLE MILK
   1 CUP LIGHT CREAM
      SWEETENED MASCARPONE (PAGE 209)

Preheat the oven to 350°F. Butter a 9 x 13-inch baking pan.

Peel, core, and cut the apples into large slices. Place them in a large bowl, squeeze the juice of 1 lemon over them, dust with the nutmeg, and toss with 3 tablespoons of sugar.

In a small saucepan over low heat, melt the butter. In a large bowl, combine half of the butter and ¼ cup of the sugar. Mix in ¾ cup of the walnuts, the juice of the other lemon, and the cider or water. Combine this with the apple chunks and the bread cubes. Pour the apple and bread mixture into the baking dish.

In a medium bowl, beat together the remaining 6 tablespoons butter and ¼ cup of the sugar. Whisk in the eggs, then the milk and cream. Pour evenly over the apples and bread. Sprinkle the top with the remaining tablespoon of sugar, some nutmeg, and the remaining ¼ cup walnuts. Bake for 45 minutes, or until the bread and nuts are toasty and golden. Taste to make sure the apples are cooked. Allow to rest for 15 minutes.

Serve warm with sweetened mascarpone.

I'm surprised that the knotty little apples I find at the Saturday market have intense flavor. Even our long-neglected apple trees bravely put forth their scrawny crop. Too tiny to slice, they at least make a respectable apple butter. For this husky dessert, cut good, hard apples into chunky slices. Use a loaf of day-old country bread; fresh bread would be too soft.

Gone are the days when red and yellow Delicious ruled our choices in the United States. At my market in North Carolina, I can select from a dozen varieties. Granny Smith is still a good choice for baking, but try these new old flavors: Honeycrisp, Braeburn, Empire, or Arkansas Black.

Serve this with gelato, if you prefer.

TWO CRUSTS FOR TARTS

PASTA FROLLA

MAKES ONE 10- TO 12-INCH PIECRUST PLUS DOUGH
FOR LATTICE TOP

Frolla means "friable." The origin is from the Latin *friabilis,* "to crumble." Use this crust when you want a texture similar to shortbread. *Pasta frolla* is always used for a *crostata.* I like it for lemon and fruit tarts and for the classic Torta della Nonna, grandmother's tarts (page 197).

Any leftover dough can be baked as cookies with a couple of pine nuts on each, or with a dab of jam on top.

2¼ CUPS ALL-PURPOSE FLOUR, SIFTED, PLUS
    ADDITIONAL FOR PREPARATION
½ CUP SUGAR
    PINCH OF SALT
8 TABLESPOONS (1 STICK) UNSALTED BUTTER,
    ROOM TEMPERATURE
1 WHOLE EGG PLUS 1 YOLK, LIGHTLY BEATEN
    ZEST OF 1 LEMON

Mound the flour, sugar, and salt on a work surface. Make a well, with the butter and eggs in the center. With your hands or two forks, blend in the butter and eggs until the mixture looks like breadcrumbs. Add the zest. Knead, forming a soft dough. If you use a food processor, the butter should be cold and cut in bits. Pulse together the butter, sugar, and salt. Add the eggs and lemon zest, pulse 1 to 2 times, and then add the flour ½ cup at a time, pulsing, just to blend, until the dough forms.

Form the dough into a disk, pat it with flour, and wrap it with a damp dishtowel. Chill for at least 2 hours.

Flour a cool surface, divide the dough in half, and roll out a circle of dough to fit your pie plate. Flip the pastry over the rolling pin and into the pie plate. Or simply press the pastry into the pan with your fingers. Use leftover disk of dough for a lattice top, or form a long twisted coil to fit around the rim. Crimp the edges or press them with fork tines.

FLAKY PASTRY

MAKES ONE 10- TO 12-INCH PIECRUST

For a folded, rustic tart, Apple in a Cage (page 199), or anything savory, this is the crust to choose. It's tender and buttery, but not at all fragile. I find that two tablespoons of water is usually enough, but for some flours, or on a humid day, you might need a little less or more.

1½	CUPS ALL-PURPOSE FLOUR, PLUS ADDITIONAL FOR PREPARATION
¼	TEASPOON SALT
4	TABLESPOONS SUGAR (OMIT FOR A SAVORY CRUST)
12	TABLESPOONS (1½ STICKS) UNSALTED BUTTER, ROOM TEMPERATURE
1	LARGE EGG, BEATEN
2 TO 4	TABLESPOONS COLD WATER

Combine the flour, salt, and sugar in a large bowl or mound them on a work surface. Work in the butter and egg with a fork until the mixture takes on the look of breadcrumbs. Add cold water if needed to form a soft dough. Or, with a food processor and using cold butter cut in bits, follow the same order, pulsing just enough to mix in each ingredient. When a mass begins to develop, remove the dough.

Form the dough into a disk, pat it with some flour, and wrap it in a damp dishtowel. Chill for at least an hour.

Generously flour a cool surface and roll out a circle of pastry to fit your pie plate. Flip the pastry over the rolling pin into the pie plate. Crimp the edges together to make it pretty. Chill again while you make the filling.

FOLDED FRUIT TART
with MASCARPONE

SERVES 6

FLAKY PASTRY (OPPOSITE)
1 CUP (8 OUNCES) MASCARPONE
¼ CUP SUGAR
12 MINT LEAVES, TORN
¼ CUP SLICED ALMONDS, TOASTED
6 LARGE PEACHES, PEELED, PITTED, AND SLICED INTO EIGHTHS
4 TABLESPOONS (½ STICK) UNSALTED BUTTER, IN PIECES

Preheat the oven to 375°F.

On a generously floured surface, roll out the crust 3 inches larger in diameter than you normally do for a pie plate. Flip it over the rolling pin, and slide it onto a parchment-lined baking sheet.

In a large bowl, combine the mascarpone, sugar, mint, and almonds. Fold the peaches in very gently. Pile the mixture into the center of the pastry, dot the peaches with butter, and flop the edges of the crust over, pressing them down a bit into the fruit. Don't seal the top—leave a 4- or 5-inch hole. Bake for about 20 minutes or until the pastry is golden and the peaches have softened.

I first learned to make folded piecrusts long ago from a Paula Wolfert cookbook. On a cookie sheet, you spread the crust, pile the filling in the middle, and then loosely flap the edges toward the center, forming a rustic tart with a spontaneous look.

Florio Malvasia delle Lipari, made by Duca di Salaparuta, will provide the right accent for the tastes of almonds and peaches.

Silvia's RICOTTA TART

SERVES 8

Silvia's ricotta *torta* often appears on the menu at Il Falconiere. A magnificent dessert for a holiday dinner, it compares to cheesecake as the waltz to the tango. You can enhance the *torta* with golden raisins plumped in grappa or cognac; lightly toasted sliced almonds or pine nuts; dried cherries plumped in *vin santo*; or some slivers of fine-quality candied citron. I use a fluted French-style tart pan with a removable bottom.

FOR THE PASTRY
- ½ CUP (1 STICK) UNSALTED BUTTER, SOFTENED
- ¼ CUP SUGAR
- 1 EGG
- 1¾ CUPS ALL-PURPOSE FLOUR, SIFTED
- PINCH OF SALT
- ½ TEASPOON GROUND CINNAMON

FOR THE FILLING
- 2 CUPS WHOLE MILK
- ZEST OF 1 LEMON OR ORANGE
- 4 EGGS
- ⅔ CUP SUGAR
- PINCH OF SALT
- 1 TABLESPOON FLOUR
- 2 CUPS (1 POUND) FRESH RICOTTA, PREFERABLY FROM SHEEP OR GOAT MILK
- 1 TEASPOON VANILLA EXTRACT

Make the pastry. Cream the butter and sugar in a large bowl. Add the egg and beat until light and fluffy. Gradually add 1 cup of the flour, the salt, and cinnamon, stirring to combine well. Sprinkle in the rest of the flour, and mix until the dough is easy to handle. Turn it out onto a floured surface and knead briefly. The dough will be very soft. Shape it into a round disk, cover with plastic wrap, and refrigerate for at least 1 hour or overnight.

Preheat the oven to 350°F.

Make the filling. In the bottom of a double boiler, bring water to a boil and then turn the heat down to a good simmer. Put the milk in the top of the double boiler with the zest, and heat thoroughly; do not let it boil. Set aside.

Combine 3 of the eggs with the sugar in a large bowl and whisk until a thick ribbon forms. Incorporate the salt and the flour. Add a small amount of the milk into the egg mixture to temper it, then slowly beat the egg mixture into the milk. Cook it over the simmering water, stirring, for about 10 minutes, or until it is thicker than heavy cream but not as thick as sour cream. Remove from the heat; pour it into the bowl to cool.

Roll out the dough to fit a 12-inch tart pan. Line the pan and prick the bottom and sides with a fork. Bake for 10 minutes and then remove it from the oven.

In a small bowl, whip the ricotta with a fork. Fold it into the filling. Mix well, and then stir in the remaining egg and the vanilla. Beat thoroughly. Pour the filling into the prepared pastry shell. Bake for 35 minutes, or until the filling is firmly set.

TORTA *della* NONNA

FOR THE FILLING

1/3	CUP ALL-PURPOSE FLOUR
1 1/2	TEASPOONS CORNSTARCH
2 1/2	CUPS WHOLE MILK
4	EGG YOLKS, BEATEN
2/3	CUP GRANULATED SUGAR
	ZEST AND JUICE OF 1 LEMON
1	TEASPOON VANILLA EXTRACT

FOR THE TORTA

	PASTA FROLLA (PAGE 192), CHILLED
1	TEASPOON POLENTA
1/3	CUP PINE NUTS, LIGHTLY TOASTED
2	TABLESPOONS CONFECTIONERS' SUGAR

Grandmother's tart—homey but rich. *Pinoli*—pine nuts—are essential. Once I garnered my own from the pine trees lining our driveway. Blackened fingers and several broken nails later, I decided that particular sustainable practice would have to go. This is a lovely, simple dessert, one that spells Tuscany.

Make the filling. Sift the flour and cornstarch into a small bowl. In a medium saucepan, whisk together the milk, egg yolks, granulated sugar, and zest. Over medium heat, stir for 5 to 8 minutes, or until slightly thickened. Turn the heat to medium low, and slowly add the flour and cornstarch, whisking all along. When it becomes a very thick and creamy custard, about 2 minutes, stir in the lemon juice and vanilla. Remove from the heat, set aside, and allow to cool while you prepare the pastry.

Preheat the oven to 350°F.

Divide the chilled dough in half and, on a well-floured surface, roll out one half to fit a 10-inch tart pan. Keep the other half of the dough covered and chilled. Sprinkle half of the polenta into the bottom of the crust. Pour in the filling, then roll out the other circle of dough to cover, and crimp it around the overlapping edges. Press the pine nuts into the dough and sprinkle with the remaining polenta. Bake for about 35 minutes, or until the crust and nuts are bronzed. Remove the torta and let it rest for 5 minutes before sifting the confectioners' sugar over the top . Serve warm.

Ivan's Big BLACKBERRY CROSTATA

SERVES 12 TO 14

We once wondered why you see so many jars of fruit preserves in Italy, a country that doesn't have a toast-and-jam breakfast culture. We learned the jars of apricot, blackberry, raspberry, quince, fig, and plum are for *crostata*, that default, hands-down number one dessert of Tuscany. Ivan gathers wild blackberries in early September, and makes the jam. His jewel-colored jams seem to contain summer. We serve his fig jam with cheeses and his quince jam with roasts.

For pastry and pasta, Ivan, like almost all Tuscan cooks, uses a *spianatoia*, a 2 x 3-foot board, with a lip that keeps it steady on the counter.

His *pasta frolla* is a little different from Gilda's (page 194). Use any fruit jam with a homemade texture. It's best to make this by hand because of the quantities.

3 CUPS ALL-PURPOSE FLOUR, PLUS EXTRA FOR THE WORK SURFACE
1 EGG AND 2 EGG YOLKS
¾ CUP SUGAR
12 TABLESPOONS (1½ STICKS) UNSALTED BUTTER, ROOM TEMPERATURE, PLUS ADDITIONAL FOR THE BAKING DISH
ZEST OF 1 LEMON
3 TABLESPOONS *VIN SANTO*
¼ TEASPOON SALT
2 CUPS BLACKBERRY JAM

Mound the flour in a large bowl or on a countertop. Make a well in the center and drop in the eggs and sugar. Start to work the mixture with your fingers or a fork, then add small bits of the butter, the lemon zest, wine, and salt, blending everything. On a floured surface, form the pastry into 2 disks—using about ¾ of the dough in one—and allow it to rest in the refrigerator, wrapped in a damp cloth, for at least 2 hours.

Preheat the oven to 350°F.

Working quickly, roll out the large disk of dough and fit it into a 12- to 14-inch pan with low sides. Spread the blackberry jam over the pastry. Roll out the rest of the dough, cut it into ½-inch strips, and make a lattice over the jam. Bake for 30 to 35 minutes. The pastry will look toasty.

APPLE *in a* CAGE

SERVES 8

- 1 CUP WALNUT HALVES, GROUND
- ½ CUP PLUS 2 TABLESPOONS SUGAR
- 3 TABLESPOONS UNSALTED BUTTER, SOFTENED, PLUS 2 TABLESPOONS MELTED
- 1 TEASPOON GROUND CINNAMON
- 8 BAKING APPLES, PEELED AND CORED ALL-PURPOSE FLOUR, FOR THE WORK SURFACE FLAKY PASTRY (PAGE 194; RECIPE DOUBLED)
- 8 CLOVES
- 1 CUP HEAVY CREAM

Mele in Gabbia—the apple is sweetly imprisoned in a crossover cage of pastry, a playful dessert that is as much fun to see as to taste. Choose baking apples, such as Granny Smiths or Rome.

Preheat the oven to 400°F.

In a small bowl, combine the walnuts, ½ cup sugar, 3 tablespoons softened butter, and ½ teaspoon of the cinnamon. Fill each apple core with 3 tablespoons of the mixture.

On a generously floured surface, roll out the pastry and cut 3-inch-wide strips that are long enough to wrap around the apples, about 8 inches. Using two strips of pastry, cross them to make an *X* for each apple. Place the apple upside down in the center and fold the pastry around it. Press the pastry snugly to the apple. On a parchment-lined baking sheet, arrange the apples upright, so that the foldover seam of the pastry is on the bottom. Press a clove into the top of each for beauty's sake. Chill 30 minutes.

Brush the pastry with the melted butter and bake for 30 minutes, or until the pastry is crusty and browned and the apples are softened.

Meanwhile, whip the cream with the remaining 2 tablespoons of sugar and ½ teaspoon of cinnamon. Serve the hot apples immediately and pass the cream.

RASPBERRY ALMOND ROULADE

SERVES 8

This lavish roulade makes me happy. When I see it, I remember all the fabulous pastry shops in Palermo with their windows filled with candied citron, glacéed fruit, marzipan, and fanciful cakes. Because the rosy roulade looks festive, I love to carry it to the table, anticipating the "ahs" that will ensue.

FOR THE CAKE

¾ CUP SUPERFINE SUGAR
   JUICE AND ZEST OF 1 LEMON
3 EGGS, SEPARATED
¾ CUP ALL-PURPOSE FLOUR
2 TEASPOONS BAKING POWDER
⅛ TEASPOON SALT
⅛ TEASPOON CREAM OF TARTAR
   BUTTER FOR THE BAKING PAN
2 TABLESPOONS CONFECTIONERS' SUGAR

FOR THE FILLING

2 CUPS FRESH RASPBERRIES
2 TABLESPOONS SUPERFINE SUGAR
2 CUPS HEAVY CREAM
¼ CUP SLICED ALMONDS, TOASTED

Preheat the oven to 325°F.

Make the cake. In a large bowl or food processor, mix well the superfine sugar and zest. Add the yolks one at a time and beat or pulse until the egg mixture is pale and light. Stir in the lemon juice. Sift the flour and baking powder into a small bowl and then whisk or pulse them, a third at a time, into the sugar and eggs. In a separate medium bowl, beat the egg whites with the salt and cream of tartar until they form stiff waves. In fourths, fold them into the yolk mixture, pulsing only once or twice if you're using the processor.

Butter a 17 x 13-inch pan with low sides and line it with parchment, buttering that as well. Spread the batter evenly—it will be somewhat thin—and bake for 15 to 18 minutes or until golden and just set. Allow the cake to cool for 5 minutes.

Invert the pan onto a sheet of parchment (or a dishtowel) sprinkled with half of the confectioners' sugar. Peel back the top parchment and sift the remaining confectioners' sugar onto the cake.

While the cake is in the oven, make the berry filling. In a small saucepan over medium-low heat, cook ½ cup of the raspberries with 1 tablespoon of the sugar for about 5 minutes, pressing the berries with a spoon so that they release their juices. Press the berries and their juices through a strainer. Set aside, discarding the pulp.

In a large bowl, whip the cream, adding the remaining tablespoon of superfine sugar gradually. The cream should hold a peak. Divide the whipped cream in half. Into one half, fold the berry liquid and the remaining 1½ cups of raspberries. Spread this on top of the cake, smoothing it to the edges of the long sides and to 1 inch from the edges on the short side. Lifting the cake by the parchment or dishtowel, slowly roll the narrow end forward. With two spatulas, transfer the roulade to a serving plate. Spread over the top the remaining whipped cream and scatter on the almonds.

Serve the roulade right away, or it can wait 2 or 3 hours in the fridge. To cover it with plastic wrap, stand up four or five tall toothpicks or skewers in the cake so the wrap doesn't touch the cream.

FIG *and* WALNUT TART

SERVES 10

	PASTA FROLLA (PAGE 192)
10	LARGE FRESH FIGS, HALVED
	EXTRA-VIRGIN OLIVE OIL, FOR THE BAKING SHEET
6	TABLESPOONS HONEY (JASMINE OR LAVENDER, IF AVAILABLE)
5	TABLESPOONS SUGAR
1	CUP WALNUT HALVES, TOASTED AND HALVED AGAIN
½	CUP HEAVY CREAM
2	TABLESPOONS ALL-PURPOSE FLOUR
¼	TEASPOON FRESH THYME LEAVES OR ⅛ TEASPOON DRIED

Preheat the oven to 375°F.

Place the pastry in a 10- or 12-inch pie plate, trim the edges, pierce it all around with fork tines, and pre-bake for 5 minutes. Remove from the oven and set aside.

Raise the oven control to broil. Line a baking sheet with parchment paper and oil the paper. Arrange the figs on the paper and drizzle 2 tablespoons of honey and 2 tablespoons of sugar over them. Broil 2 to 4 minutes. Let the figs sizzle a moment, slightly caramelizing them. Don't let the sugar brown—just melt. Remove them from the oven and turn down the oven temperature to 350°F.

In a small pan over medium-low heat, melt 1 tablespoon of sugar. Add the walnus and toss just to coat them, about 1 minute. Take care: sugar can so easily turn rock hard. Remove the walnuts to a plate to cool.

Place the figs cut side up in the piecrust and arrange the nuts evenly over them. In a small bowl, mix well the cream, remaining ¼ cup honey, the flour, thyme, and remaining 2 tablespoons sugar. Spoon evenly over the figs. Bake 25 minutes, or until the crust is golden and the filling is warmly browned.

Figs grow all over the Mediterranean world, wild on hillsides, cultivated in gardens, and volunteering through cracks in dusty parking lots. When they're ripe, there's a plethora of figs. Wrap them with prosciutto, put up fig preserves, serve them with cheeses, roast figs with duck, stuff them with crushed amaretti cookies and mascarpone—and still there are figs. But they're ephemeral: suddenly they are gone for another year. *Carpe diem*—seize the day and try them in the homey but elegant form of this tart.

Massimo and Daniela's WINE CAKE

SERVES 8

Massimo and Daniela preside over Bar Tuscher in a venerable palazzo in Cortona. All the expats in town are lured by their house-made desserts and the intimate tables, so perfect for a private conversation away from the piazza. When I walk into town in the mornings, I'm assured of a quiet spot for writing in my notebook. Although I'm torn between their warm *cornetti* filled with berries and this tender *vin santo*–scented cake, the cake usually wins.

- 1 CUP (2 STICKS) PLUS 5 TABLESPOONS UNSALTED BUTTER, SOFTENED, PLUS ADDITIONAL FOR THE PAN
- 1⅓ CUPS SUGAR
- 1⅓ CUPS (11 OUNCES) WHOLE-MILK RICOTTA
- 3 EGGS
- ⅓ CUP *VIN SANTO*
- 1⅓ CUPS ALL-PURPOSE FLOUR, PLUS ADDITIONAL FOR THE PAN
- 2 TEASPOONS BAKING POWDER
- 2 TABLESPOONS PINE NUTS, TOASTED
- 1 TO 2 TABLESPOONS CONFECTIONERS' SUGAR

Preheat the oven to 350°F. Butter and lightly flour a nonstick 9-inch springform tube pan or 10-inch tube pan.

In a large bowl, combine the butter, sugar, and ricotta until fluffy. Beat in the eggs one at a time and then incorporate the *vin santo*. Sift the flour and baking powder into a small bowl, then slowly and thoroughly beat them into the batter. Pour into the prepared pan, sprinkle the pine nuts on top, and bake for 30 minutes, or until the cake is firm but springy to the touch and a promising aroma fills the kitchen. Cool before removing the cake from the pan. Sift confectioners' sugar over the top.

Ed's CANTUCCI

MAKES 50 TO 55 COOKIES

These cookies are sold in the United States as "biscotti," but *biscotti* just means "cookies." The particular name is *cantucci*. The *primo biscotto* in Italy, *cantucci* traditionally are served with *vin santo*. Both in Italy and the United States, they can be tooth-cracking hard, and no wonder: they've been trapped in cellophane for months. They do keep well but are not immortal. Fresh *cantucci* are nutty, crunchy but yielding, and with a faint tang of lemon.

12 TABLESPOONS (1½ STICKS) UNSALTED BUTTER, MELTED, PLUS ADDITIONAL FOR THE COOKIE SHEETS
3 EGGS, BEATEN, PLUS 1 BEATEN YOLK FOR A WASH
ZEST OF 1 LEMON
1 TABLESPOON FENNEL SEEDS
2 CUPS SUGAR
4 CUPS ALL-PURPOSE FLOUR
1½ TEASPOONS BAKING POWDER
PINCH OF SALT
2 CUPS SLICED ALMONDS

In a large bowl, mix well the butter, 3 eggs, zest, fennel seeds, and sugar. Combine the flour, baking powder, and salt in a sifter and sift about ½ cup at a time into the butter mixture, blending well before adding more. Mix in the almonds.

Slightly knead the dough with your hands until it comes together. Form the dough into two logs no more than 2 inches wide. Wrap in plastic and chill for 1 hour.

Preheat the oven to 375°F. Butter two parchment-lined cookie sheets.

Place the logs on one sheet. Brush each with some of the beaten yolk for browning. Bake for 18 to 20 minutes. Remove the logs to a work surface, and let them rest for 10 minutes. Slice them into cookies ½ inch thick. Arrange them on the two sheets, and return them to the oven for 5 to 7 more minutes, or until they are cooked through in the middle. Serve warm, or cool and store in tight-lidded tins. Don't overbake—you don't want those tooth-breakers.

Il Falconiere's CHOCOLATE CAKE *with* VANILLA SAUCE

SERVES 10

- 1 CUP (2 STICKS) UNSALTED BUTTER, PLUS ADDITIONAL FOR THE RAMEKINS
- 1 CUP SUPERFINE SUGAR
- 4 EGGS
- 3 TABLESPOONS RUM (OR TIA MARIA)
- 2 TABLESPOONS ESPRESSO OR STRONG COFFEE
- ¾ CUP ALL-PURPOSE FLOUR, PLUS ADDITIONAL FOR THE RAMEKINS
- 1 TABLESPOON PLUS 1 TEASPOON BAKING POWDER
- ½ CUP HIGH-QUALITY UNSWEETENED COCOA POWDER
- 4 FIRM BUT RIPE PEARS, PEELED, CORED, AND DICED

FOR THE VANILLA SAUCE

- 1 QUART HEAVY CREAM
- ½ VANILLA BEAN, SPLIT
- 8 EGG YOLKS
- 5 TABLESPOONS SUPERFINE SUGAR
  SOLID CHOCOLATE BAR FOR MAKING CURLS, OR CHOCOLATE-COVERED COFFEE BEANS

With this dessert, Silvia suggests a full-bodied sweet red wine with enough alcohol to "clean your mouth." Most wonderful with chocolate is Duca Di Salaparuta, Ala Liquor-vino Amarascato, a velvety, wild-cherry–based dessert wine with a hint of almonds.

Preheat the oven to 250°F. Butter and flour ten 3½-inch ramekins and set aside. Bring a kettle of water to a boil.

In a large bowl, beat the butter and sugar to a soft cream. Beat in the 4 eggs one at a time. Stir in the rum and coffee. Sift the flour, baking powder, and cocoa together in a separate small bowl, and then in fourths, incorporate this into the batter.

Gently fold in the pears. Pour into the ramekins, filling each halfway. Place the ramekins in a 13 x 15-inch baking dish or whatever size your oven accommodates. Fill the dish halfway with boiling water. Bake the cakes for 10 minutes, then increase the temperature to 350°F and continue baking until set, about 15 minutes more.

Make the vanilla sauce. In a heavy 2- or 3-quart saucepan over medium-high heat, bring the cream and vanilla bean almost to a boil, and cook for 2 to 3 minutes. Quickly reduce the heat to medium low. In a small bowl, thoroughly beat together the yolks and sugar. Whisk the eggs into the cream and continue cooking on low heat, stirring continuously, for 5 to 6 minutes, until the mixture has the consistency of whipped cream. Remove the vanilla. The sauce can rest in the fridge; if you're serving it later, gently reheat.

Unmold the ramekins onto individual plates, or serve the cakes in the ramekins. Spoon warm vanilla sauce over the tops, and garnish with curls of chocolate (made with a vegetable peeler or cheese slicer) or chocolate-covered coffee beans.

CHERRIES STEEPED
in RED WINE

- 1½ CUPS RED WINE
- 1 POUND CHERRIES, PITTED
-    ZEST OF 1 LEMON
- 1 TABLESPOON SUGAR
-    SWEETENED WHIPPED CREAM OR SWEETENED MASCARPONE (RECIPE FOLLOWS)

In a medium saucepan, bring the wine to a boil, and then add the cherries, lemon zest, and sugar. Reduce the heat immediately to simmer for 15 minutes, stirring occasionally. Cover the cherries and let them stand for 2 or 3 hours. Serve in bowls with plenty of the wine juice and a dollop of the whipped cream or mascarpone.

All through June we buy sweet-tart cherries by the kilo and start eating them in the car on the way home. Almost nothing you can invent improves on the taste of a ripe, plump cherry. We've planted eight trees, but the birds are willing to eat them about a week before they're ripe, leaving us half-pecked fruit. I tried hanging old CDs from the branches, hoping the glitter would scare the birds away. Instead, they seem attracted to the flashes, darting even faster among the branches, and screeching with excitement.

With these, I like to serve thin slices of lemon cake (see photograph, page 211).

SWEETENED MASCARPONE

An alternative to whipped cream, sweetened mascarpone adds a grace note of complexity to fruits. The tangy sweetness of mascarpone, sugar, and cream also suits many tarts and cakes. It's quicker than, and not as sweet as, whipped cream, and can be made several hours ahead.

MAKES 12 SERVINGS

- 1 CUP (8 OUNCES) MASCARPONE
- ½ CUP HEAVY CREAM
- 4 TABLESPOONS SUGAR
-    ZEST OF 1 LEMON OR ORANGE (OPTIONAL)

In a small bowl, mix everything with a fork until smooth.

LEMON CAKE

A family import, this Southern cake is one I serve poolside in Tuscany with gelato and fireside with glasses of Barolo Chinato, or, privately, for breakfast. Slender slices seem at home with Lemon Hazelnut Gelato or Cherries Steeped in Red Wine (pages 182 and 209).

1 CUP (2 STICKS) UNSALTED BUTTER, ROOM TEMPERATURE, PLUS ADDITIONAL FOR THE PAN
2 CUPS SUGAR
3 EGGS
3 CUPS ALL-PURPOSE FLOUR, PLUS ADDITIONAL FOR THE PAN
1 TEASPOON BAKING POWDER
¼ TEASPOON SALT
1 CUP BUTTERMILK, OR LIGHT CREAM PLUS 1 TABLESPOON LEMON JUICE
3 TABLESPOONS LEMON JUICE, PLUS ZEST OF 1 LEMON

FOR THE GLAZE AND GARNISH
1½ CUPS CONFECTIONERS' SUGAR, SIFTED
4 TABLESPOONS (½ STICK) UNSALTED BUTTER, SOFTENED
3 TABLESPOONS LEMON JUICE
TINY CURLS OF LEMON PEEL

Preheat the oven to 325°F. Butter a nonstick 10-inch tube or Bundt pan, then lightly flour it.

In a large bowl, cream together the butter and sugar. Beat in the eggs one at a time; the mixture should be pale and light. Into a medium bowl, sift together the flour, baking powder, and salt. Incorporate the flour mixture into the butter mixture alternating with the buttermilk and beginning and ending with the flour mixture. Beat in the lemon juice and zest. Pour into the prepared pan and bake for 50 to 55 minutes. The cake is done when a toothpick inserted into the center comes out clean and the cake is firm but springy to the touch.

Make the glaze. In a medium bowl, beat the confectioners' sugar into the butter and lemon juice. Mix until supple and spreadable. Smooth it over the cooled cake, and decorate with the lemon peel.

APERITIVI E DIGESTIVI

NOCINO *217*

RICCARDO'S LIMONCELLO *217*

Bitter is a popular taste in Italy. All those herbal after-dinner drinks and *aperitivi*, collectively known as *amari*, bitters, that the Italians knock back are definitely an acquired taste. "Italians seem to have *acquired* more tastes than many of us," Ed observes.

—FROM *Bella Tuscany*

Fanfare and finale—*aperitivi* and *digestivi* set the mood and close the curtain on a Tuscan meal. I love the mystery and romance of these fragrant, spicy, or bitter elixirs. The home cook usually has two or three family recipes for *digestivi* and literally hundreds are commercially available. The recipes for limoncello and nocino that we're including will make you feel like a master-distiller.

At every party, prosecco, that airy, fulsome sparkling wine, flows freely while fried zucchini blossoms and crostini are passed. Sometimes we add a spoon of white peach juice for a Bellini. The prosecco grape grows up north in the Veneto and Friuli, but its wine is *the aperitivo* all over Italy. At our house, we usually pour Bellavista spumante or Bisol prosecco, but there are many to choose from. We think cold prosecco is best dry, rather than sweet. Around Tuscan homes, you don't find much else offered as an *aperitivo*,

although in bars someone might order a Campari soda, a Negroni, Campari on the rocks, or a dry Cinzano with a twist. The cocktail trend just hasn't caught on in the country, I suppose, because of the deep-rooted custom that drinks and food go together. Usually in rural Tuscany, when we arrive at someone's home for dinner, we go straight to the table, but after the long *cena*, dinner, we linger long over *digestivi*.

Monks made these special concoctions from time immemorial. Looking for cures, looking for "the water of life," possibly looking for a little heady intoxication to warm them as they knelt on cold stone chapel floors, they used anything on their grounds: roots, honey, citrus, bark, plants. You can get a sense of the early pharmacy by visiting Officina Profumo Farmaceutica di Santa Maria

Novella, in Florence. The monastery complex's nearby pharmacy is known now for its soaps and lotions, but look on their product list and you'll find the remedies ("Antique Preparations") and liqueurs that the Dominicans started making in the thirteenth century. The handed-down formulas still prevail. Tuscans keep a stash of *digestivi* and bring them out with a flourish at the end of dinner.

Especially on summer nights, we hate for the evening to end. At our table, when the plates are cleared, Ed brings out the *vin santo* and the grappa and the Averna: the Tuscan after-dinner triumvirate. *Vin santo* is a *passito* made from partially dried grapes; grappa is a distilled wine; Averna is an *amaro,* a bitter. The bitters, such as Montenegro, Cynar, and Fernet Branca, make up most of what are collectively called *digestivi.* Tuscans really appreciate bitter tastes, from field salads to all kinds of greens to the *digestivo* at the end of a dinner. Even prosecco has a faint apostrophe of bitterness amid its effervescence.

A wedge of pecorino, a bunch of grapes, or a handful of walnuts might still be on the table, but at this point, who eats? A thimbleful of a *digestivo* simply closes the circle on dinner. If there are *stranieri,* foreigners, at the table, I'll bring out the limoncello, too. (I've never seen a Tuscan choose limoncello.) *Digestivi* are strong juju. Maybe they simply start a brushfire in your stomach and that's where the digestive aspect comes in. One sip and your eyes widen, your throat feels like a telephone is ringing in it. I can't; Ed can. I'll join the *americani* with a little limon-cello with a splash of fizzy water.

Even if *digestivi* scald a wimpy palate like mine, I like to sip as the others toss back a glug or two. Each *digestivo* continues to send out concentric circles of tastes and in the meditative after-dinner languor, we can discuss endlessly what scents and herbs are reverberating all the way to our toes. Dried orange peels, lemon balm, myrtle, mint, cinnamon, rose hips, anise, rue, muscat, borage—some *digestivi* have seventy or so herbs and plants.

These are some of the *digestivi* we stock at Bramasole:

- *Averna.* Always, Averna. Ed's male friends all belong to the Averna cult. It's made in Sicily from thirty-two herbs.
- *Fernet Branca.* This must have begun as a medicine. Yes, it's bitter and its ingredients—beet sugars, myrrh, saffron—many find to be a cherished acquired taste.
- *Cynar.* An artichoke base.
- *Strega.* This is sunflower yellow and tastes of anise. Over seventy herbs are used as well.
- *Frangelico.* A sip of this is delicious with tarts. It's made from hazelnuts, vanilla, cocoa, and orange blossoms. How could it not be delightful?
- *Barolo Chinato.* A favorite. Barolo wine reined in by quinine to remind you that life is bitter.

- *Sambuca.* This comes from elderberry, the same source as my great-aunt's homemade wine, which my father refused to drink because he feared it would make him go blind.
- *Nocino.* A profound and intense brew from walnuts.
- *Limoncello.* A few sips and you long for Sorrento. I like to add a tablespoon to a glass of lemonade. Some people are in love with this and drink three or four glasses because it seems innocent. This is a mistake.
- *Amaretto.* The translation: little bitter. The almond taste actually comes from apricot pits. The recipe also includes grapes and herbs, as it has since it was invented in Saronno in 1525.
- *Grappa.* Excellent grappa is distilled elegance. Country home brew can singe the roof of your mouth. Go for the best. Tuscans love grappa.
- *Vin Santo.* A dark amber *passito* with glints of gold, it tastes like liquid firelight, or as though time has melted into a glass. One of the greatest is made near us at Avignonesi Vineyards. It's a pleasure to see their grape-drying room after the harvest, when the grapes are spread on racks lining a long room. In old farmhouses, grapes were dried on nails driven along ceiling beams. All over Tuscany, if you stop anywhere for a visit, you'll inevitably be offered *vin santo* and *cantucci.* Many people still make their own *vin santo,* some quite smooth and nutty. This most-loved and convivial drink may have roots as holy wine, as the name implies. By now, it is ubiquitous.

NOCINO

MAKES 2 PINTS

- 20 UNSHELLED GREEN WALNUTS
- 3 CUPS SUGAR
- 1 QUART ALCOHOL, 90 PROOF, OR VODKA
- 1 STICK CINNAMON
- 4 CLOVES

Cut the walnuts into quarters. Protect your hands with gloves because even green walnuts stain. In a large sterilized jar with a lid, combine the walnuts, sugar, alcohol, cinnamon, and cloves. Close and shake to mix well. Store for 2 months, shaking the jar every once in a while. Then let it sit for another 2 months. At the end of 4 months, remove the walnuts and discard them. Filter the liquid through cheesecloth into sterilized bottles and cork them. This *digestivo* will keep for several years in a dark cabinet.

Traditionally, green walnuts are gathered on June 24, San Giovanni's day. As far as I know, they're used only for preparing this shadowy and spicy elixir.

This recipe belongs to Giuseppe Frangieh, who runs the hotel restaurant Corys in Cortona.

Riccardo's LIMONCELLO

- 8 ORGANIC LEMONS—RICCARDO STRESSES THAT THE LEMONS MUST BE PURE
- 1 QUART ALCOHOL, 90 PROOF, OR VODKA
- 2 CUPS SUGAR
- 1 QUART BOTTLED STILL WATER

Peel the lemons, leaving a little pith attached to the peel. Reserve the lemons for another use. Put the peels and alcohol in a large sterilized jar with a lid. Close it tightly and leave it in a cool place for four to seven days. Gently shake it a couple of times a day. The peels will lose their brilliant yellow color.

On the fifth day, or later, in a large saucepan, heat the sugar and water almost to the boiling point but not quite. Reduce the heat, and simmer and stir for 5 minutes. Allow the syrup to cool.

Strain the lemon-scented alcohol through gauze or a strainer into the sugar syrupage Discard the peels. Whisk the mixture well and pour into 4 sterilized pint bottles. Let the limoncello sit for two days. Later, you can store it indefinitely in the freezer, so it will be frosty-cold when you serve it in small glasses.

When life gives you lemons, make limoncello. Paolo Castelli, who owns Trattoria Dardano, makes a potent non-lemon version with bay leaves. We tease him and call it his medicine. Aurora makes her own *finocchiocello* with fennel. Riccardo Baracchi, who is a fabulous winemaker, still makes his own limoncello. I was taught by my friend Lucio to add four lemon leaves to the alcohol and peel mixture, to deepen the color.

A FINAL LIBATION NOTE

Water is always on the table. The unwritten rule is to refill your water glass as often as your wine glass—your consumption will be perfect.

After a meal, espresso is the other essential. Even at the olive grove, the men have a portable burner so they can relax after we eat. Since Ed is a coffee fanatic, at home our guests are served a strong, restricted potion napped with perfect toasty gold *crema*. It's the exclamation point to the evening. No one seems bothered by caffeine at midnight. Ed maintains that espresso gives him the strength to sleep. Guests seem to agree. A quick nip, a little lick of the lips for the last spot of *crema*, and you're out the door. Another splendid evening at the table in Tuscany.

ACKNOWLEDGMENTS

Thanks begin with a neighbor's gift of plums on the first day we arrived and end with a roasted guinea hen at a friend's house on the last day of this summer. In between, many, many feasts—thank you to all our Italian friends and those from many other countries who have sat at our table and invited us to theirs. The dedication of this book (pages 4 and 5) continues in my mind for many more pages. Particular thanks to friends Alberto Alfonso, Placido Cardinali, the Di Rosa family, Susan Swan, and Franca Dotti. *Grazie* to Riccardo Barrachi, Antonio Moretti, and Giampaolo Venica, fabulous winemakers, and to everyone at Il Falconiere, Corys, and Pane e Vino. Marco Molesini of Enoteca Molesini forever gives us great wine recommendations.

We're honored to be published by Clarkson Potter. Our editor, Aliza Fogelson, lavished her attention on the project and provided intelligent guidance and good cheer throughout the process. The clean and elegant design comes from the visionary Marysarah Quinn. Our thanks to the whole enthusiastic team at Clarkson Potter. For the quintessential Tuscan photographs, Steven Rothfeld has our eternal thanks. We had a marvelous time during his six visits to Bramasole. All photographs in the book were taken in Tuscany and I am so grateful to Steven for traveling with us to antique fairs, the Maremma, and out-of-the-way spots in pursuit of the authentic. We were joined twice by Kim Sunée, who helped us with recipe testing and styling. She was also great fun to be with. *Mille grazie*, too, to Madeline Granara Heinbockel and Melissa Vaughn for recipe testing and helpful information.

I'll set a beautiful table for Frances Gravely and Susan Gravely any time. The Gravelys own Vietri and generously offered us Italian dinnerware, which supplemented my own collection. Not only that, at the end, Fernando Manetti, their representative in Italy, said we should keep all the dishes! *Che fortuna!* Our great gratitude for their friendship and generosity. Their designs enliven pages 6, 62–63, 87, 110–111, 116, 125, 132, 148, 150–151, and 198.

Peter Ginsberg has been my agent for ten books. To him—and to everyone at Curtis Brown Ltd.—enormous thanks for all. And the same to my friends at Steven Barclay Agency. What luck to work with these two superb groups. Good luck, too, to continue to work with my editor at Broadway Books, Charlie Conrad, who comes each summer with his family to visit us.

This book includes photographs of many friends. Thanks to all of you for gracing our pages. Jacket: Ed, Cecilia Cascella, Fulvio Di Rosa, Frances, Silvia Regi, Riccardo Baracchi; page 11: Franco Mechelli; page 14: Annetta Burbi; page 15: Luigi Camerini, Fabio Pelucchini, Albano Fabrizi, with Ed; page 33: Riccardo Giannini at Frantoio Oleario Giancarlo Giannini; page 39: Claudio Lunghini; page 56: Roberto Spensierati; page 104: Friends at Bramasole; page 114: Ed, Fiorella Badini, Placido Cardinali, Frances; page 122: Palma Tribbioli and her son Dario Paolelli; page 132: Chiara Cardinali; page 140: Papero Di Donato with Ed and Frances; page 158: Albano Fabrizi; page 185: Beppe Agnolucci and friends at Bar Torreone, Cortona; page 186: Giacomo Vanelli; page 205: Daniela Ottonello and Massimo Olivieri; page 218: Aldo Cipri, Riccardo Baracchi, Ed, and Benedetto Baracchi at Locanda del Molino.

Other photograph identifications: page 11: Women at a goose feast near Cortona; page 16–17: Ghirlandaio fresco, Santa Maria Novella, Bramasole Olive Oil; page 19: vintage cookware at Locanda del Molino, Cortona; page 25: Tasting balsamic vinegar from the cask; page 26 below: Borgo di Vagli in fog, Cortona; page 29: Bramasole garden; page 36: near Pienza; page 39: Pecorino with bay leaves; page 80: At Trattoria Pane e Vino, Cortona; page 107: Bread oven at Fonte delle Foglie; page 115: Borgo di Vagli, Cortona; page 135: Montepulciano; page 143: bulletin board in fishermen's kitchen—see Marcello Mastroianni! page 171: Cortona; page 173: Val D'Orcia; page 208: Apostle, from Ghirlandaio's *Last Supper* in Ognissanti, Florence; page 212: Enoteca Molesini wine tasting in Cortona; page 215: Osteria del Teatro, Cortona. All other food and table settings were taken at our houses, Bramasole or Fonte delle Foglie.

Back in the U.S.A., Ashley, Peter, and Willie have feasted and appreciated almost every recipe in our repertoire. We've loved cooking with Susan Wyler. Thank you all.

INDEX

Note: Page references in *italics* indicate photographs.

A

Almond(s)
    Cream, Peaches with, 190
    Ed's Cantucci, 206, *206*
    Franca's Sea Bass, *146*, 147
    Raspberry Roulade, 200–201
Anchovies
    and Breadcrumbs, Pici with, Pane e
        Vino's, 80, *80*
    preserved, buying, 29
Aperitivi and *digestivi*
    about, 214–17
    Nocino, 218
    Riccardo's Limoncello, 218–19
Apple
    Bread Pudding, Rustic, 191
    in a Cage, 199, *199*
Artichokes
    and Cherry Tomatoes, Little Veal
        Meatballs with, 128, *128*
    Fried, 50, *51*
    and Potatoes, Fava Beans with, 161
    Rolled Veal Scallops Filled with,
        127
    Sun-Dried Tomatoes, and
        Chickpeas, Chicken with, 118–19,
        119
    and Tomatoes, Baked, 157
    When-in-Rome, *52*, 53
Arugula
    and Pancetta, Ann Cornelisen's Pasta
        with, 81
    Pesto, 43
Asparagus
    Four Other Roasted Vegetables, 163,
        164–65
    Risotto Primavera, *101*, 103

B

Bacon. *See* Pancetta
Balsamic Vinegar, 25
Basics
    Balsamic Vinegar, 25
    Besciamella, 24
    Brine, 25
    Dried Cannellini Beans and
        Chickpeas, 24
    Focaccia, 23
    Gilda's Salt, 24
    Pesto, 26
    Soffritto, 20–21
    Tomato Sauce, 21
Basil
    Angry Pasta, 84
    Caprese, 58
    Ivan's Pizza Margherita, *105*, 106
    and Mint *Sorbetto*, 184, *184*
    Pesto, 26
    Trenette with Pesto and Potatoes, 72
    Zucchini with Lemon Pesto, 168
Bean(s). *See also* Green Beans
    Cannellini, and Sage Topping, 44, *45*
    cannellini, cooking, 24
    Chicken with Artichokes, Sun-Dried
        Tomatoes, and Chickpeas, 118–19,
        119
    chickpeas, cooking, 24
    Fava, Fresh, Pici with, 78–79, *79*
    Fava, with Potatoes and Artichokes, 161
    Prawns and Cherry Tomatoes with
        Purée of Cannellini, 148, *148*
    Ribollita, 98
    Salad with Chickpeas, Sun-Dried
        Tomato, and Grilled Shrimp, 174
    White, Kale, and Sausage Soup, 100,
        100
Beef. *See also* Veal
    Giusi's *Ragù*, 70, *71*
    Placido's Steak, 131
    Rolled Bresaola, 58
    Short Ribs, Tuscan Style, 129
    Tenderloin with Balsamic Vinegar, 135
Berries, Three, Tulip Shells with, 189
Besciamella, 24
Blackberry Crostata, Ivan's Big, 198, *198*
Breads and bread-based dishes
    Bruschette and *Crostini*, 40, 41–47
    Focaccia, 23
    Onion Soup in the Arezzo Style, 99
    Pappa al Pomodoro, 96
    Rustic Apple Bread Pudding, 191
Bresaola, Rolled, 58
Brine, 25
Brodetto, 145
Bruschette and *Crostini*, 40, 41–47

C

Cakes
    Chocolate, Il Falconiere's, with
        Vanilla Sauce, 207
    Lemon, 210
    Raspberry Almond Roulade, 200–201
    Wine, Massimo and Daniela's, 204,
        205
Caponata, 54
Caprese, 58
Carrots
    Fascicles of Summer Vegetables, 170
    Risotto Primavera, *101*, 103
    Soffritto, 20–21
Celery
    Soffritto, 20–21
Chard with Raisins and Orange Peel,
    173
Cheese(s)
    Baked Peppers with Ricotta and Basil,
        152, 156
    Caprese, 58

Folded Fruit Tart with Mascarpone, 195, *195*

Four, and Sausage, Baked Pasta with, *90,* 91

Giusi's Eggplant Parmigiana, 139

Ivan's Pear Agnolotti with Gorgonzola and Walnuts, 73, *75*

Ivan's Pizza Margherita, *105,* 106

Lasagne with *Ragù,* 88

mozzarella, notes about, 28

Onion Soup in the Arezzo Style, 99

Pecorino and Nut Topping, 46

Pizza with Caramelized Onion and Sausage, 107

Polenta with Sausage and Fontina, 138

Rich Polenta Parmigiana with Funghi Porcini, *136,* 137

Risotto Saltato, 104

Rolled Bresaola, 58

Silvia's Ricotta Tart, 196

Sweetened Mascarpone, 209

Three, and Shrimp, Pasta Shells with, 82

Wild Mushroom Lasagne, 89

Cherries Steeped in Red Wine, 209, *211*

Chestnuts in Red Wine, 172

Chicken
with Artichokes, Sun-Dried Tomatoes, and Chickpeas, 118–19, *119*
Under a Brick, *116,* 116–17
with Olives and Tomatoes, 117
Patrizia's Rabbit, 121

Chicken livers
Ed's *Crostini Neri,* 47

Chocolate Cake, Il Falconiere's, with Vanilla Sauce, 207

Citrus zest, note about, 29

Clementine *Sorbetto,* 185

Cookies
Ed's Cantucci, 206, *206*
Tulip Shells with Three Berries, 189

Crab and Lemon, Spaghetti with, 85

Crostini and *Bruschette, 40,* 41–47

D

Duck Sauce, Silvia's Pasta with, 76–77

E

Eggplant
Caponata, 54
Involtini, 166, *167*

Parmigiana, Giusi's, 139
Roasted Vegetables, Especially Fennel, 162

Eggs
Pasta Frittata, 139
Sformati, 160, *160*

Equipment notes, 19–20

F

Farro Salad, 57

Fennel
and Citrus, Rolled Sole with, 144
and Citrus Salad, 175, *175*
Honey-Glazed Pork Tenderloin with, 124
Roasted, 162

Fig and Walnut Tart, 201

Fish. *See also* Shellfish
Brodetto, 145
Fisherman's, for Lunch, 143
Franca's Sea Bass, *146,* 147
Fritto Misto, 140, *141*
Pane e Vino's Pici with Breadcrumbs and Anchovies, 80, *80*
preserved anchovies, buying, 29
Rolled Sole with Fennel and Citrus, 144
Sea Bass in a Salt Crust, 142

Flaky Pastry, 194

Flan, Garlic, 158

Focaccia, 23

Fritto Misto, 140, *141*

G

Garlic
and Citrus Peel, Baked Olives with, 55
Flan, 158
Gilda's Salt, 24
Roasted, Topping, 46
Soup, 94

Garnishes, 29

Gelato
Lemon Hazelnut, 182, *182*
Peach, 183

Grains. *See also* Risotto
Farro Salad, 57
Polenta with Sausage and Fontina, 138
Rich Polenta Parmigiana with Funghi Porcini, *136,* 137

Green Beans
with Black Olives, 159, *159*
Fascicles of Summer Vegetables, 170

Four Other Roasted Vegetables, 163, *164–65*

Trenette with Pesto and Potatoes, 72

Greens
Ann Cornelisen's Pasta with Arugula and Pancetta, 81
Arugula Pesto, 43
Chard with Raisins and Orange Peel, 173
Grilled Red Radicchio, 43
Kale, White Bean, and Sausage Soup, 100, *100*
Minestrone: Big Soup, 97
Salad with Chickpeas, Sun-Dried Tomato, and Grilled Shrimp, 174

H

Ham. *See also* Prosciutto
Savory Round Zucchini, 169, *169*

Hazelnut Lemon Gelato, 182, *182*

I

Ingredient notes, 18–19, 28–32

K

Kale, White Bean, and Sausage Soup, 100, *100*

L

Lamb
Chops, "Finger-Burner," *132,* 133
Roast Leg of, with Herbs and Pancetta, 134

Lemon(s)
Cake, 210
and Crab, Spaghetti with, 85
Hazelnut Gelato, 182, *182*
organic, buying, 29
Pesto, Zucchini with, 168
Riccardo's Limoncello, 218–19

Limoncello, Riccardo's, 218–19

Liver
Ed's *Crostini Neri,* 47

M

Meatballs, Little Veal, with Artichokes and Cherry Tomatoes, 128, *128*

Melon, Prosciutto and, 58

Minestrone: Big Soup, 97

Mint and Basil *Sorbetto,* 184, *184*

Mushroom(s)
dried porcini, working with, 28

Mushroom(s) (*continued*)
  Rich Polenta Parmigiana with Funghi
    Porcini, *136*, 137
  Wild, Lasagne, 89
Mussels
  Star of the Sea *Gratinato*, 60

N

Nocino, 218
Nut(s). *See also* Almond(s); Walnut(s)
  Chestnuts in Red Wine, 172
  Lemon Hazelnut Gelato, 182, *182*
  and Pecorino Topping, 46
  Torta Della Nonna, 197

O

Olive oil, extra-virgin, about, 14, 31–32
Olive(s)
  all'Ascolana, 56
  Angry Pasta, 84
  Baked, with Citrus Peel and Garlic, 55
  Black, Green Beans with, 159, *159*
  Caponata, 54
  Franca's Sea Bass, *146*, 147
  Quite Spicy, 55
  and Tomatoes, Chicken with, 117
Onion(s)
  Caramelized, and Sausage, Pizza
    with, 107
  Soffritto, 20–21
  Soup in the Arezzo Style, 99
Orange(s)
  Fennel and Citrus Salad, 175, *175*
  organic, buying, 29
  Peel and Raisins, Chard with, 173
  Rolled Sole with Fennel and Citrus,
    144

P

Pancetta
  and Arugula, Ann Cornelisen's Pasta
    with, 81
  and Herbs, Roast Leg of Lamb with,
    134
  Smoky Pasta, 83
Panini, favorite combinations for, 23
Panna Cotta, 187
Pasta
  Angry, 84
  with Arugula and Pancetta, Ann
    Cornelisen's, 81
  Baked, with Sausage and Four
    Cheeses, 90, 91

Basic, 68–69
cooking directions, 69
with Duck Sauce, Silvia's, 76–77
Frittata, 139
Gnocchi di Patate, 93
Ivan's Pear Agnolotti with Gorgonzola
  and Walnuts, 73, *75*
Lasagne with *Ragù*, 88
Orecchiette with Shrimp, 77
Pane e Vino's Pici with Breadcrumbs
  and Anchovies, 80, *80*
Pici with Fresh Fava Beans, 78–79, *79*
Potato Ravioli with Zucchini, Speck,
  and Pecorino, 86–87, *87*
Semolina Gnocchi, 92, *92*
serving sizes, 69
Shells with Shrimp and Three
  Cheeses, 82
Smoky, 83
Spaghetti with Lemon and Crab, 85
Trenette with Pesto and Potatoes,
  72
Wild Mushroom Lasagne, 89
Pastry
  Flaky, 194
  Pasta Frolla, 192
Peach(es)
  with Almond Cream, 190
  Folded Fruit Tart with Mascarpone,
    195, *195*
  Gelato, 183
  Sacred, 190
Pear(s)
  Agnolotti with Gorgonzola and
    Walnuts, Ivan's, 73, *75*
  Il Falconiere's Chocolate Cake with
    Vanilla Sauce, 207
  Winter, in Vino Nobile, 188
Pea(s)
  Orecchiette with Shrimp, 77
  Risotto Primavera, *101*, 103
  and Shallot Topping, 44, *45*
Pepper(s)
  Baked, with Ricotta and Basil, *152*, 156
  Baked Tomatoes and Artichokes, 157
  Fascicles of Summer Vegetables, 170
  Quite Spicy Olives, 55
  Red, Melted with Balsamic Vinegar,
    47
  Red, Tart, Fiorella's, 59, *59*
  Roasted Vegetables, Especially
    Fennel, 162
  Yellow and Red, Soup, 95

Pesto, 26
  Arugula, 43
  Lemon, Zucchini with, 168
  and Potatoes, Trenette with, 72
Pine nuts
  Torta Della Nonna, 197
Pizza
  with Caramelized Onion and Sausage,
    107
  Margherita, Ivan's, *105*, 106
Polenta
  Parmigiana, Rich, with Funghi
    Porcini, *136*, 137
  with Sausage and Fontina, 138
Pork. *See also* Ham; Pancetta
  Giusi's *Ragù*, 70, *71*
  Patrizia's Rabbit, 121
  Roast, Ed's, 125, *125*
  Tenderloin, Honey-Glazed, with
    Fennel, 124
Potato(es)
  and Artichokes, Fava Beans with, 161
  Gnocchi di Patate, 93
  and Pesto, Trenette with, 72
  Ravioli with Zucchini, Speck, and
    Pecorino, 86–87, *87*
  Rosemary, Domenica's, 171
Prawns and Cherry Tomatoes with
  Purée of Cannellini, 148, *148*
Prosciutto
  Eggplant Involtini, 166, *167*
  and Melon, 58
  Potato Ravioli with Zucchini, Speck,
    and Pecorino, 86–87, *87*

Q

Quail Braised with Juniper Berries and
  Pancetta, 120

R

Rabbit
  Patrizia's, 121
  with Tomatoes and Balsamic Vinegar,
    123
Radicchio, Red, Grilled, 43
Raisins and Orange Peel, Chard with,
  173
Raspberry Almond Roulade, 200–201
Ribollita, 98
Rice. *See* Risotto
Risotto
  flavor combinations, 101
  Primavera, *101*, 103

Saltato, 104
Shrimp, 102
Rosemary
    Gilda's Salt, 24
    Potatoes, Domenica's, 171

S
Saffron, about, 28, 61
Sage
    and Cannellini Bean Topping, 44,
        45
    Gilda's Salt, 24
    Leaves, Fried, 49
Salad(s)
    Caprese, 58
    with Chickpeas, Sun-Dried Tomato,
        and Grilled Shrimp, 174
    Farro, 57
    Fennel and Citrus, 175, 175
    Shrimp, Frances's Summer, 149
Salt, Gilda's, 24
Sauces
    Besciamella, 24
    Giusi's Ragù, 70, 71
    Tomato, 21
Sausage(s)
    and Caramelized Onion, Pizza with,
        107
    and Fontina, Polenta with, 138
    and Four Cheeses, Baked Pasta with,
        90, 91
    Kale, and White Bean Soup, 100, 100
    Olive all'Ascolana, 56
Sea Bass
    Franca's, 146, 147
    in a Salt Crust, 142
Semifreddo, Strawberry, 186
Semolina Gnocchi, 92, 92
Shallot and Pea Topping, 44, 45
Shellfish. See also Shrimp
    Brodetto, 145
    Fritto Misto, 140, 141
    Prawns and Cherry Tomatoes with
        Purée of Cannellini, 148, 148
    Spaghetti with Lemon and Crab, 85
    Star of the Sea Gratinato, 60
Shrimp
    Grilled, Chickpeas, and Sun-Dried
        Tomato, Salad with, 174
    Orecchiette with, 77
    Prawns and Cherry Tomatoes with
        Purée of Cannellini, 148, 148
    Risotto, 102

Salad, Frances's Summer, 149
Star of the Sea Gratinato, 60
and Three Cheeses, Pasta Shells with,
    82
Soffritto, 20–21
Sole, Rolled, with Fennel and Citrus,
    144
Sorbetto
    Basil and Mint, 184, 184
    Clementine, 185
Soups
    Garlic, 94
    Kale, White Bean, and Sausage, 100,
        100
    Minestrone: Big Soup, 97
    Onion, in the Arezzo Style, 99
    Pappa al Pomodoro, 96
    Ribollita, 98
    Yellow and Red Pepper, 95
Speck, Zucchini, and Pecorino, Potato
    Ravioli with, 86–87, 87
Strawberry Semifreddo, 186

T
Tangerines
    Clementine Sorbetto, 185
    Fennel and Citrus Salad, 175, 175
Tarts
    Fig and Walnut, 201
    Folded Fruit, with Mascarpone, 195,
        195
    Ivan's Big Blackberry Crostata, 198,
        198
    Red Pepper, Fiorella's, 59, 59
    Silvia's Ricotta, 196
    Torta Della Nonna, 197
Tomato(es)
    Angry Pasta, 84
    and Artichokes, Baked, 157
    and Balsamic Vinegar, Rabbit with,
        123
    Caprese, 58
    Cherry, and Artichokes, Little Veal
        Meatballs with, 128, 128
    Eggplant Involtini, 166, 167
    Giusi's Ragù, 70, 71
    Ivan's Pizza Margherita, 105, 106
    and Olives, Chicken with, 117
    Pici with Fresh Fava Beans, 78–79, 79
    Roasted, Topping, 42, 42
    Roasted Vegetables, Especially
        Fennel, 162
    Sauce, 21

Sun-Dried, Artichokes, and
    Chickpeas, Chicken with, 118–19,
    119
Tulip Shells with Three Berries, 189

V
Veal
    Meatballs, Little, with Artichokes
        and Cherry Tomatoes, 128, 128
    Ossobuco, 130
    Scallops, Rolled, Filled with
        Artichokes, 127
    Shank, Roasted, 126, 126
Vegetables. See also specific vegetables
    Minestrone: Big Soup, 97
    Ribollita, 98
    Risotto Primavera, 101, 103
    Roasted, Especially Fennel, 162
    Roasted, Four Other, 163
    Sformati, 160, 160

W
Walnut(s)
    Apple in a Cage, 199
    and Fig Tart, 201
    and Gorgonzola, Ivan's Pear Agnolotti
        with, 73, 75
    Nocino, 218
    Pecorino and Nut Topping, 46
    Polenta with Sausage and Fontina,
        138
    Rustic Apple Bread Pudding, 191
Wine
    Cake, Massimo and Daniela's, 204,
        205
    Red, Cherries Steeped in, 209, 211
    Red, Chestnuts in, 172
    Winter Pears in Vino Nobile, 188

Z
Zucchini
    Fascicles of Summer Vegetables, 170
    Fiorella's Red Pepper Tart, 59, 59
    Flowers, Fried, 48, 49
    with Lemon Pesto, 168
    Roasted Vegetables, Especially
        Fennel, 162
    Round, Savory, 169, 169
    Speck, and Pecorino, Potato Ravioli
        with, 86–87, 87

CLARKSON POTTER is a trademark and
POTTER with colophon is a registered
trademark of Random House, Inc.

Library of Congress Cataloging-in-
Publication Data
Mayes, Frances, and Edward Mayes.
   The Tuscan sun cookbook / Frances
Mayes and Edward Mayes; photographs
by Steven Rothfeld. — 1st ed.
   1. Cooking, Italian—Tuscan style.
2. Cookbooks.   I. Mayes, Edward
Kleinschmidt.   II. Title.
TX723.2.T86M394   2012
641.5955'5—dc22   2011013195

ISBN 978-0-307-88528-9
eISBN 978-0-307-95386-5

Printed in China

Design by Marysarah Quinn
Photographs by Steven Rothfeld

10 9 8 7 6 5 4 3 2 1

FIRST EDITION